Signs

A New Approach to Coincidence, Synchronicity, Guidance, Life Purpose, and God's Plan

by Robert Perry

SEMEION PRESS

ISBN 978-0-9822500-0-6

Library of Congress Control Number: 2008910954
Library of Congress subject heading:
Coincidence—Religious aspects.

Published by Semeion Press, Sedona, Arizona.
www.semeionpress.com

Cover design and layout by Phillips Associates UK Ltd

Online Help!

For news and updates on CMPEs, including
a free e-newsletter, please visit

www.semeionpress.com.

If you are interested in having a personal
sign consultation, please go to

www.semeionpress.com.

Table of Contents

Foreword

by

Barbara Harris Whitfield

This is an amazing book. Reading it is an exceptional experience. Not only will you be introduced to Robert Perry's important new model for understanding highly synchronous events, you may actually be led, as I was, into an astonishing personal encounter with the phenomenon he sets forth here. Even if you question the clarity or relevance of divine guidance when you first pick up this book, by the time you reach the last page, you're sure to open your mind to the possibility—even the likelihood—that God or the Universe has been trying to communicate with you all along. You just haven't been paying attention! That was certainly my experience as I traversed this original, imaginative, and inspired work.

This isn't the first time I've been transported from the material world to the spiritual realm. In 1975, at age thirty-two, I underwent a near-death experience (NDE) following spinal fusion surgery to correct a debilitating congenital condition. In my book about that occurrence, titled *Full Circle: The Near-Death Experience and Beyond*,[1] I chronicle the "life review" that totally changed me. My life review appeared as thousands of bubbles, each revealing a scene from my past that offered not only a glimpse of what happened and what I was feeling, but also an awareness of how others felt. I was held by a divine intelligence—God—and filled with a sense of being connected at a higher level of consciousness to everyone my life had touched.

In the years since that profound encounter, during which I've done extensive research on the aftereffects of the NDE, I believe that same Divine Intelligence has communicated with me through synchronicities that serve as arrows intentionally pointing me in a certain direction. In my latest book, *The Natural Soul*,[2] I refer to these synchronicities as "cosmic postcards," because I perceive in them that something "Higher" is signaling us.

Perry's model is more complex, bringing to the exploration of highly synchronous occurrences a depth and wisdom that extends beyond my own work and that of other researchers and writers in the field. In this book, he investigates what he calls Conjunctions of Meaningfully Parallel Events—CMPEs—referring to them less formally as "signs," but assigning the term a decidedly different meaning than usual.

As I read Perry's book and his new model unfolded in front of me, my thoughts began heading off in opposing directions. Reacting from the left side of my brain, where the part of me that reasons like a medical school psychiatry researcher resides, I thought, "Oh Boy! This could be the bridge to proving that meaningful coincidences go beyond chance."

The other side of my brain, however—the side that thrives on direct experience—went into gridlock when faced with his definitive and precise model. This was just too much to take in. I became concerned that analyzing something so sacred would only serve to secularize it and make it less profound. So I found myself resisting the concept of CMPEs, telling myself that Perry's model is too narrow in its acceptance of its own phenomena. Its rules might heedlessly negate many of the coincidences in my life—those parallel occurrences I had previously considered significant. And its interpretive methods might strip out meanings my right brain wanted to embrace. Even so, I persevered in my reading, all the while hoping for and anticipating a moment of enlightenment—a moment of really getting what this model was saying about this form of divine guidance.

My perseverance paid off! As I reached the later chapters, I was won over by the strong evidence presented by the book's examples and began to see the benefits of Perry's model. Finally, while reading the last chapter, I experienced a powerful CMPE—an undeniable sign of my very own—which Robert later confirmed and interpreted with me. Its message affirmed that CMPEs are in harmony, not in conflict, with the synchronicities that have been guiding my journey since the time of my NDE and life review.

Twenty years ago, I titled my first book *Full Circle* as an expression of what I yearned to achieve in my personal spiritual journey. I had e-mailed Robert Perry about this just hours before reading his Chapter 11 with its opening sign by the same title. This triggered that "aha" moment I had been waiting for. I contacted him to express my excitement, and he applied the guidelines from the book to do an analysis of my "sign," demonstrating to me how much more deeply his model can go in interpreting highly synchronous events.

My CMPE wasn't just an arrow pointing a way. It was a demonstration of layer upon layer of spiritual wisdom, comparable to what I learned in each revelatory scene of my life review. In fact, it felt like a remarkable continuation of that profound experience. As this wisdom moved through me, I could actually watch as my personal worldview was changing. There was a kind of domino effect that is perhaps best described as a "revelation"— a true sense of completion that answered the longing expressed in my book's title.

The sign's message, as Robert revealed it to me, became an experiential understanding of God being my partner *in this lifetime*—and patiently waiting for me to realize this. The experience of reading this book has brought me a sense of certainty that God has been with me the whole time, talking to me through synchronicities; but until now, I only saw their surface—the pointing part of the arrow. Until now, I was missing out on their deeper meanings.

I have since experienced additional CMPEs. What is most remarkable to me is that they fit exactly the model Robert describes. I am even seeing how different CMPEs are related, as explained in Chapter 7, in that two of my signs clustered together to become synergistic, demonstrating that one and one equals so much more than two.

I now see this model of CMPEs as having tremendous potential usefulness.

(1) On a personal level, they can touch each one of us by demonstrating that, although we haven't always been paying attention, God has always been talking to us, loud and clear.

(2) Based on my experience, I believe CMPEs may have valuable applications in psychotherapy, which I intend to explore in my own private practice.

(3) Scientifically, this model holds great potential. The CMPE model is

demonstrating the testable end of the synchronicity spectrum. There actually is a prospect of real research going forward about this.

I resisted this model in the beginning, and, frankly, gave Robert Perry a pretty hard time about it. I thought this model was reducing the significance of other synchronicities that didn't fit the pattern. Now I see that I can continue to honor my wonderful little cosmic postcards, while also recognizing the more encompassing capabilities of the CMPE model. At one end of the synchronicity spectrum are my small coincidences—the means by which a higher power cheerfully waves at us to get our attention. And at the other end of this spectrum are CMPEs—a cosmic DSL fiber optic line that clearly and distinctly communicates to us God's deeper broadcast.

Understanding the deeper meaning of my own CMPE catapulted me into a powerful experience of shedding any lingering remorse I accumulated during my journey. I am filled with the wonderful awareness that God is holding me, here in this life—now—just like God was holding me in my life review. We don't have to leave this world to experience this sense of being divinely cared for. It's the same on both sides. All we need do is learn to listen. This book is teaching us how.

Barbara Harris Whitfield
Atlanta, Georgia
October 2008

Introduction

The purpose of this book is to introduce a "new" phenomenon. It is not really new. I suspect it has been occurring to people throughout time. It may very well have occurred to you. However, defining its structure and characteristics, so it can be noticed, distinguished from related phenomena, and used—that's new.

Stories of this phenomenon can occasionally be found in books on synchronicity or coincidence. Indeed, if it occurs in our own lives, we probably think of it that way, if we notice it at all. However, if we could scratch beneath the surface of one of the head-turning coincidences we experience, and knew what we were looking for, we might find far more than meets the eye. We might find a phenomenon that has an astonishingly intricate design and seems to be offering wise counsel on a situation in our lives.

I have come to believe that this phenomenon has tremendous significance. That is why, after more than thirty years of private use and investigation, I have decided to share what I have learned in the form of this book. In my experience, this phenomenon can provide invaluable guidance for our lives; and what's more, it could potentially change our understanding of reality. It is endlessly fascinating.

The first half of the book (through Chapter 6) is devoted to learning what this phenomenon is and how we can make use of it in our own lives. These chapters (especially Chapters 3-6) are trying to teach us a new and unfamiliar concept. They therefore contain a good deal of explanation, but this is balanced out by examples, including a cameo story at the beginning of each chapter, and by practical exercises.

Once we have gained an understanding of what the phenomenon is, the following chapters are mainly devoted to exploring the nature of the guidance it offers. Can it predict the future? Can it see deeply into situations and people? What is its philosophy? We will explore these questions by looking at dozens of real-life examples.

Then, in the final chapter, I explore possible explanations of where it comes from and offer the conclusions I have reached.

Even though the subtitle of the book mentions "God's plan," aside from brief references in the book, for most of the book I am going to leave the God issue aside, reserving it for the final chapter. This is not a phenomenon that presumes belief in God. It is a phenomenon in its own right. It just happens, without the need for any cooperation from us. And it happens to people regardless of their belief in God. What I want us to do, therefore, is learn about it the way we would learn about any natural phenomenon: first observe it as an event and learn its characteristics, and only then turn our attention to speculation about its ultimate nature.

Chapter 1
A Meeting Point of Belief and Skepticism

The Bucket Brigade

I am the head of a small nonprofit organization called the Circle of Atonement. It is dedicated to serving students of *A Course in Miracles*, a contemporary spiritual path that utilizes forgiveness as the primary catalyst of psychological healing and spiritual awakening. As with most nonprofits, money is usually tight, and we often find ourselves wondering how we are going to pay the bills. In February 2003, we were facing a particularly serious financial crunch, so serious that we were wondering if we would need to make changes in staffing—maybe let some people go, cut back on people's hours, or institute a temporary pay cut. The way our board processes such issues is to first discuss them, then close our eyes, pen and paper in hand, and ask for guidance. What we "hear" comes in different forms. Some of us receive a flow of words, some see inner pictures, some just get an inner sense or feeling. Our ability to hear is not unusual and what we hear is not infallible. However, it is almost always wiser and more helpful than the discussion we had before we asked, and it often sends us in completely new directions.

In this particular case, the guidance of one board member—my future wife Nicola—stood out. She saw an inner picture and heard commentary that explained the picture. Here is her description of what she saw:

> I got a picture of a group of people forming a "chain gang" (where items pass quickly along the chain of people). [She saw this as happening in what we call our mailroom, where we ship out our books and tapes]. Everyone was in the exact right place in order to be a useful part of that chain. There were no over-laps, no missing people, just a united and well-functioning

group. Part of its efficiency was down to the fact that each person knew their exact spot in that chain, and that others, too, knew exactly who was where. You can't throw an object to someone if you're not sure where they are! Another part of its efficiency was simply because people were operating as a team, and everyone was joined and working together towards the same goal.

The commentary Nicola heard said that in order to form this "chain gang," we needed to reevaluate how the organization functioned. We had already chosen a focus for the year: to get our message out through publishing an introductory book.[3] Now we had to look at everything, from top to bottom, and ask ourselves how well it served that focus. We were told to reexamine the *who*—people's roles—and the *what*—the organization's activities, all in light of our larger goal. According to this guidance, we must leave no stone unturned. We needed a shakeup. We needed to shift people's roles around (the "who") and set aside certain activities (the "what"), all in order to weld ourselves into a tightly coordinated team that served a single goal.

We sensed that this challenged the whole way we had traditionally functioned. We had always stressed the importance of each individual pursuing his or her own special calling. As a result, our organization tended to do a number of disparate things at once, which were only loosely coordinated. If, then, we actually implemented this guidance, if we saw each person's function as determined by the needs of a team effort, it would turn our whole way of operating upside down.

However revolutionary the idea was, something felt right about it. While we were discussing it, I pointed out that someone else's guidance had made similar points, which seemed to lend strength to the basic idea. I also put my finger on the appropriate term for the picture Nicola had seen. She had called it a "chain gang," but she had told us that wasn't the right term—since a chain gang is a group of convicts linked together. What she saw, she said, was like the chain people form to put out a fire. It finally hit me that this was called a "bucket brigade" and I mentioned that to the group.

Shortly after I said that, something totally unexpected happened. Our meeting was taking place downstairs and we heard what sounded like falling water in a nearby room—the mailroom. We burst into that room to discover that water was literally cascading through the unfinished ceiling onto the shipping table. Without thinking, we moved the table aside and grabbed several large plastic buckets stacked next to it and arranged them in a row to catch the falling water, which happened to be pouring through the ceiling in a straight line. Staff and volunteers ran downstairs to help; they got rags and began mopping up what they could. Everyone was in motion. As it turned out, a repairman was upstairs fixing the washing machine. He had mistakenly turned the wrong knob, causing water to pour through the floor of the laundry room, which was also the ceiling of the mailroom.

Only once we returned to our meeting room and sat down to catch our breath did we realize we had just performed an eerie reenactment of the picture from Nicola's guidance. In response to a crisis, we had dropped our usual roles and activities, mobilized as a single unit, and formed a line of water-filled buckets. We had formed a bucket brigade!

Stories like this give us the sense of a higher hand at work, as if some invisible organizing principle is literally shaping physical circumstances. This naturally raises a whole host of weighty questions and thorny issues. For many of us, it is a bell that rouses two contenders from their corners, to battle it out in a match that has been going on for ages and has no end in sight.

Is there an unseen pattern in the events of our lives? Some sort of design or plan behind what looks like chaos? Or, as we sometimes fear, is it all just random chance, just atoms colliding in the void? Is the river of our lives trying to flow somewhere, or does it just meander, without any rhyme or reason? So much rides on how we answer these questions. If we say that there is some meaningful design shaping our life story, then by implication we affirm there is meaning to our existence. There is a purpose to it all, a reason we are here. Something, or maybe someone, is watching over us.

Perhaps an unseen hand is guiding us to safe harbor. If we say life's events are pure chance, then we are saying we are left alone in a random universe, adrift on a sea of meaninglessness. We brave constant high seas to desperately preserve an existence that, in the end, doesn't mean anything. There is no hidden design, nobody watching over us, and definitely no safe harbor.

If you believe in God or in some sort of spiritual worldview, these questions have probably been answered for you. Believers tend to see patterns everywhere. They see meaningful coincidences. They see synchronicities. They see answers to prayer. An illness becomes a "lesson," sent to further their growth. A person they just met was "sent" to them for a reason. A sign on the side of a passing truck becomes literally a sign from God. When they see doors close one after another, they are obviously being told to go the other way. When a job materializes long after it was hoped for, they end up realizing it was perfect timing. When a check shows up in the mail, they are sure "the universe" sent it in response to their current need. No matter how haphazard and even tragic things appear to be, they trust that all is in divine order. While they bounce around on life's spinning roulette wheel, they have the comfort of knowing they are not bouncing at random. The game is rigged—in their favor.

The skeptic, of course, looks on the same events and sees no meaningful patterns, no evidence of a higher design. He sees the same dots; he just feels no compunction to connect them. When he thinks about someone and a few seconds later that person calls, he chalks it up to the laws of probability—occasionally, that sort of thing is bound to happen. When the long-awaited job finally materializes, he wishes it had come sooner. When his friend sees profound meaning in the sign on a passing truck, he is concerned for his friend's mental stability. What believers see as virtuous faith in an invisible tapestry, he sees as a coping mechanism, a kind of emotional antacid one takes to calm one's stomach in the face of life's unsettling realities.

However uninspiring it may be, the skeptic's side deserves to be heard. This whole process of seeing patterns in life's events is incredibly subjective. Let's be honest—do we *really* know that there are meaningful patterns in the circumstances of our lives? And even if the patterns are actually there, how can we be certain about what they mean? When the skeptic says it's all chance, do we have a genuinely good argument with which to counter him? Haven't you noticed that the patterns we see out there aren't particularly convincing unless one is already a believer, unless one doesn't *need* convincing? In seeing an intelligent hand at work in our lives, might we not be like the dog who reacts to the vacuum cleaner as if it's an intelligent being? Can we, just for the sake of argument, admit the possibility that we are seeing not real patterns, but merely the projection of our own deep need for order and meaning and safety?

These considerations are bolstered by an experiment published in *New Scientist* in 2002. This experiment was conducted by Peter Brugger, a neuroscientist from Zurich, Switzerland, to test his observation that "people who believe in the paranormal often seem to be more willing to see patterns or relationships between events where skeptics perceive nothing."[4] Brugger took twenty believers and twenty skeptics and rapidly flashed on a screen before them a series of real faces and scrambled faces. Then he flashed a series of real words and made-up words. The job of his subjects was to tell the real faces and words from their phony counterparts. As predicted, the believers were much more likely to see a face or word when there wasn't one. In other words, they were prone to seeing patterns that simply weren't there.

Yet, to be fair, the believer's side needs to be heard, too. Some amazing things happen in this world, things that seem so coincidental, so intelligently designed, that explaining them away requires its own kind of faith—faith in nothingness. Think of the story with which I began this chapter. In both events—Nicola's guidance and the water leak—there is a crisis at the Circle of Atonement, in response to which we drop our usual roles and activities, mobilize as a single unit, and form a bucket brigade, a line of water-filled buckets. What are the odds of two events with that much in common just happening to collide in time and space? Can we honestly explain it away by saying that, according to the laws of probability, things like this are bound to happen occasionally? Unquestionably, the believer's mind sometimes sees patterns that aren't there, but could it also be that the skeptic's mind overlooks patterns that *are* there? Significantly, this is exactly what Brugger found in his experiment: The skeptics were more likely to miss real faces and real words that flashed across the screen.

There does appear to be truth on both sides of the fence, and this leaves most of us painfully torn between the two. We have our more analytic side, which wants things to be carefully tested, and which listens when science tells us, for instance, not to breathe asbestos. But most of us also have our believer side, which believes in all sorts of spiritual realities and truths that have no scientific support, and which is quite willing to see certain events as "meant to be"—as evidence of some higher hand at work. These two sides operate by completely different rules, which makes it quite uncomfortable when, despite our best efforts, they actually meet.

What we really need is a way to make peace between these two sides. As a step in this direction, what would be ideal is a phenomenon that actually meets the criteria of our more scientific, analytic side, and which, having done so, then provides concrete evidence that there *is* a pattern to life's events, there is a plan. Wouldn't it be wonderful to find a phenomenon that shows that, in the midst of all the apparent randomness, we can objectively see a larger purpose at work?

Why synchronicity does not go far enough

If you are a believer, no matter what sort of believer, you probably see instances in your life of what is called synchronicity. Synchronicity is a term coined by psychiatrist Carl Jung to describe the spontaneous coming together in time of events that seem to be meaningfully related. It is roughly the same thing we often mean by "coincidence." Jung saw synchronicities as evidence of an acausal principle at work, whereby events came together not because of the usual physical causes, but purely because they shared a similar meaning.

Jung's most famous example was that of the scarab beetle. A patient of his told him "a dream in which she was given a golden scarab,"[5] "a costly piece of jewelry."[6] Just as she is relating this dream, Jung hears a large flying insect tapping at the window.

> I opened the window immediately and caught the insect in the
> air as it flew in. It was a scarabaeid beetle...whose gold-green

colour most nearly resembles that of a golden scarab. I handed the beetle to my patient with the words, 'Here is your scarab.'"[7]

This story has been told and retold precisely because it is so remarkable. At the very moment that Jung's patient is talking about receiving a golden scarab, an actual gold-green scarab beetle comes tapping at the window. In hearing the story, most of us have the immediate feeling that something out of the ordinary happened. Jung clearly did. According to him, the arrival of the scarab was just what was needed to break through his patient's hyper-rational defense system and allow her treatment to proceed with more satisfactory results. He even pointed out that "the scarab is a classic example of a rebirth symbol."[8]

But can we really be confident that something out of the ordinary happened? Jung must have listened to untold thousands of dreams from his patients. Assuming that the average dream contained a number of items, there must have been tens or even hundreds of thousands of chances for one of those items to randomly show up while the dream was being recounted. I fully admit the story may well have been an example of an acausal ordering principle at work. It certainly has that feeling. But how can we know? How can we be truly confident? The skeptical explanation— "something like this was bound to happen sooner or later"—is, let's face it, eminently reasonable. Given that, are stories like this compelling enough to require us to invent a whole additional "acausal" principle behind the rough and tumble of physical events? Personally, I doubt it.

Unfortunately, most stories of synchronicity are weaker. At least in Jung's story, there were two events (the telling of the dream, the appearance of the beetle) that happened together in time and shared the same specific element (a golden scarab). Many stories of synchronicity, however, fall well outside this specific model, often making them even easier to explain as the results of normal probability.

In some stories, rather than two distinct events, there is one event that happens somewhere in the middle of an ongoing situation. For example, in the midst of a very painful relationship, a friend of mine picked up a hitchhiker, who began telling him about a relationship he was in. Like my friend's, the hitchhiker's relationship wasn't working. Further, in both relationships, one partner was significantly younger than the other, had a young daughter, and was battling with inner demons and suicidal impulses. The similarities seemed uncanny. Yet my friend's relationship had been going on for months, giving him countless opportunities to run into someone with a similar situation. Given that, why would we assume that this encounter was more than pure chance?

In other stories, the events are not simultaneous, but are separated by years. In the most famous example, the French writer Émile Deschamps, between 1805 and 1832, was either offered or ordered plum pudding on three different occasions, and each time a stranger named Monsieur de Fontgibu happened to be present. These stories can be impressive, but in what sense can events that are years apart be called *synchronous*?

In still other stories, the two events have no specific commonality (such as the golden scarab). Instead, the connection between them is far more subjective. For example, I might be thinking about whether to take action against an employee who has embezzled money (a fictitious situation, I might add), and at that moment the Beatles' song "Let It Be" comes on the radio. The two events have nothing objective in common. I just assume that the first event is the question and the second is the answer. But how do I know?

That is my problem with synchronicity as we usually understand it. We can't know. We cannot really be confident that something genuinely outside of the normal laws of cause and effect is operating. The alternative explanation—that probability dictates that such things are bound to happen occasionally—is just too plausible.

CMPEs

What we need, I believe, is a form of synchronicity that puts all these concerns to rest. The phenomenon I am presenting in this book, in my opinion, does just that. You could see it as a subset of synchronicity, a sort of super-synchronicity in which the skeptical explanation becomes extremely strained.

This phenomenon starts with the tighter model we saw in Jung's scarab story. It requires two distinct events that occur together in time, seemingly by chance. The two events don't need to be simultaneous, but they do need to occur within hours of each other. And they need to share an objective similarity, or parallel, as I call it, like the golden scarab in Jung's story. Yet this phenomenon goes much further than the scarab story, for here the two events need to share not *one* parallel, but rather a *list* of parallels. And this list needs to form an integrated whole, so that the two events really share an organized *complex* of parallels. At this point, the phenomenon becomes immensely more difficult to explain as the product of chance.

The phenomenon I am presenting, which I call "CMPEs" (*Conjunctions of Meaningfully Parallel Events*) or "signs" (I'll explain both terms shortly), is described by the following four-point model.

1. Events

> At least two distinct events that occur within hours of each other and that, seemingly by chance, are strikingly similar.

This, of course, is what we see with Jung's scarab story. Two events (and sometimes more) just happen to come together in time while being uncannily similar. This, however, is just the beginning.

2. Parallels

> A list of a number of elements that are shared by both events

As I said earlier, the events need to *share actual common elements* (or parallels). They cannot just be *interpreted* as being related, with one event being seen as the question and the other as the answer. Most important of all, the list of parallels needs to be fairly long. One parallel is not nearly enough. There needs to be a number of them. On average, there should be about eight, though sometimes there will be as many as thirty. Furthermore, the parallels need to come together to describe a single situation, to tell a single story. All of this will become much clearer as we go.

3. Subject situation

> *A situation of personal relevance that the CMPE is commenting on*

A CMPE is designed to say something. It is designed to comment on a situation in our lives. This situation is what I call the *subject situation*. There are rules for finding what it is, and we'll discuss those rules in Chapter 5, but the rules are really just common sense. They describe a process we usually carry out intuitively and instantly.

4. Interpretation

> *Commentary on the subject situation that arises from drawing out the "voice" of the CMPE itself*

The interpretation, of course, is what the CMPE means. To be precise, it is what the CMPE is saying about the subject situation. In Chapter 6, I will explain how this interpretation is derived, but the important thing to stress now is that it is rule-based. The interpretation is not merely a projection of our assumptions and expectations, but rather is inherent in the CMPE itself. This means that two interpreters, working completely independently, can and should arrive at basically the same interpretation.

Here is a brief definition that incorporates all four points:

> A CMPE (or "sign") consists of at least two events occurring within hours of each other that, seemingly by chance, are strikingly similar—they share an impressive list of parallels. Through the relationship between the two events, the CMPE highlights a situation in our lives and communicates a definite perspective on that situation.

As I said, I call these occurrences "signs." Unfortunately, this is a misleading use of the word, because it is so different from the usual meaning. Normally, a "sign" is a single attention-grabbing event which seems somehow portentous, as if it's carrying a message for us, such as seeing a rainbow, a shooting star, or a wild animal. Clearly, my usage of the word *sign* is very different than that. Instead of one unusual event, my "signs" consist of two events, which are often quite ordinary, yet which share a number of parallels. This difference is so great that I doubt that *any* sign in the usual sense would qualify as a "sign" in *my* sense. The fact remains, though, that I still like using the word, for the simple reason that I believe my signs do convey a message. That, as we'll see, is their essential nature.

Please understand, then, that whenever I use the word *sign*, I am using it *in my special sense, not* in the normal sense. I hope that over time you will grow accustomed to this special sense.

To honor the specific and distinct nature of this phenomenon, I also refer to it using the acronym CMPE, which stands for *Conjunction of Meaningfully Parallel Events.*

- *Events* means that you need at least two distinct events.
- *Conjunction* refers to these events coming together *in time*.
- *Parallel* means that these events share a number of objective commonalities.
- *Meaningful* means that the parallel nature of the events is designed to say something meaningful to us, something relevant for our lives.

In other words, a CMPE is a *conjunction* in time of at least two distinct *events*. These events share a number of *parallels*, and these parallels are designed to say something *meaningful* about a situation in our lives.

Do they happen to you?

This, quite naturally, is one of the first questions that occurs to people as they encounter this concept. Actually, most people say something like, "It sounds fascinating, but they just don't happen to me."

What I have learned, however, is that without the model I am presenting, any CMPEs that do happen to you will almost certainly go unnoticed. They may not go *entirely* unnoticed. You may well note an odd similarity between two events and mentally say, "Huh. That's weird." But then you will almost inevitably leave it at that. As a result, within a short time the incident will be forgotten, so that when you look back you will see no trace of CMPEs ever happening to you.

It is easy for us to notice a striking coincidence, where two events share a single obvious parallel, like Jung's scarab beetle. But a CMPE requires a whole host of *additional* parallels surrounding that initial one. These are not as immediately visible; you have to look for them. And without the model I am presenting, you have no reason to do so.

In the end, the model describes a multifaceted phenomenon. As a result, without the model this phenomenon can pass right in front of your eyes without you seeing it. This, of course, is true of a great many things in the world. Think of all the psychological disorders that went largely unnoticed until someone pulled all the symptoms together, realized they met in a single disorder, and gave the disorder a name. People were still having the disorder, but without the concept, it was hard to spot and harder to treat. It is the same with CMPEs. People *are* having them, but without the model, they are hard to spot and harder to make use of.

To return to my original question: Do they happen to you? My experience is that CMPEs are relatively infrequent. They don't happen every day. Some people I know have many of them per year. Others don't appear to have them at all. Yet even these very vague estimates from the small sample of people I know is not reliable, since it's complicated by the near certainty that signs are passing by unnoticed.

What I can say is this: Occasionally, I will try to help people I know with particular major issues with which they are struggling. Invariably, I tell them it would be ideal if we could get a sign about this issue. Once I explain the concept of signs, they will usually say, "But I don't think that happens to me." I tell them, however, to keep on the lookout for one and share with me any potential instances. As the weeks and months pass, they will often tell me about a number of occurrences that don't qualify as CMPEs. But usually, sooner or later, they will have a bonafide CMPE, maybe several. It might take months, but it usually happens. When it does, it is great to see. Now that they are armed with the model, they are able to notice the CMPEs that have surely been happening to them all along.

Although I don't know if CMPEs happen to you or not, I do think it is very possible, perhaps even likely, that they do and are simply passing by unnoticed. The main thing is for you to be on the lookout for them. When you notice a strange parallel between two events of the same day, don't dismiss it. Don't just say, "Huh. That's weird," and move on. Instead, bring all of your attention to bear on what just happened, then run it through the model using the information I will supply in the coming chapters.

The purposes of this book

I am trying to fulfill two purposes in writing this book. The first is to make this phenomenon known. This is a real phenomenon. It deserves to be studied. It deserves to be in the public eye. Its implications are potentially revolutionary. CMPEs have immense riches to give humanity both in terms of the guidance they have to offer and in terms of what their existence implies about the nature of reality. In the end, they offer concrete evidence for the existence of a higher plan for human life, and, in my view, even for the existence of a higher Planner (I'll discuss these points in the final chapter).

The second purpose is to show you how to work with your own signs. This second purpose is perhaps of greater interest to you, and understandably so. We all want guidance for our lives. My own interest in signs has first and foremost been about obtaining guidance for my own life. However, before I make too many promises about this dimension of the book, a few qualifiers are in order.

First, as I said above, I believe genuine CMPEs are fairly rare. Second, as I also said, I am convinced that most of them go unnoticed. Third, sign interpretation can be tricky. It takes knowledge of and respect for the rules. It takes the deft hand of experience. And it takes a willingness to let the rules generate interpretations that are not necessarily to your liking, which is perhaps the most challenging aspect of all.

For these reasons, even though I will attempt to teach you how to work with signs in this book, I would caution you against making big decisions based on the signs you receive. See yourself as learning a new language. As an analogy, imagine you are just learning how to speak Spanish and you hear someone across a room say a few words in Spanish. However, you are not sure if it was actually Spanish or maybe a similar-sounding language. You think you know what she said (assuming it was Spanish), although if questioned you would admit to being uncertain. Would you want to make an important life decision based on this communication? You would probably want to wait until you were more fluent in this new language, and until you had heard this person repeat whatever she said. The same thing is true of signs. One of the great things about them, in fact, is that if one sign comes along and speaks to a certain situation, others will almost certainly come along and repeat and clarify its message.

On a less cautious note, there are signs whose message is absolutely unmistakable. Even if you have just begun to learn Spanish, if a native speaker looks directly at you, shakes his head, and says, "No!" you know exactly what he means. However, for more complex communications, as well as big decisions, you will want to keep your interpretations tentative until you have gained more fluency.

While you read, then, try to keep both purposes in mind. You are learning about a phenomenon with implications for the nature of reality. And you are learning how to work with this phenomenon in your own personal life.

A sign about the preceding section

Amazingly, while I was about two-thirds of the way through the preceding section, I had a sign about it! This will give you a feel for the four-point model in action. It will also provide a window onto the experience of having a sign. This whole phenomenon can seem strange and inscrutable until the day that a sign happens to you, and while this sign obviously didn't happen to you directly, it does involve you, because it speaks to what this book is meant to do for you, the reader.

To appreciate the sign, you need to know that the content of the above section has been on my mind for about three years, during which time Nicola and I have had many discussions about it. At first, I was adamant that this book would not contain a how-to component at all. My concern was that a book—any book—simply couldn't provide adequate training in sign interpretation. I felt that interaction with a live teacher was needed. To imply that I am providing adequate training in this book—which I would do by the mere act of including instructions—seemed irresponsible. In my view, it would be like giving people the illusion that they had been adequately trained in how to drive an eighteen-wheeler, when in fact they hadn't. At that point, the "trainer" would be partly responsible for whatever the truck destroyed. I imagined hearing horror stories like, "I left my wife and five small children and began hitchhiking around the country because of a sign."

However, I slowly became convinced that the how-to component had to be in here. Signs, after all, are not some phenomenon "out there." They come to us personally, touching down in our lives with the purpose of providing guidance for those lives. Further, I gradually came to feel that a how-to component *could* be communicated in book form, at least more effectively than I had assumed (though I still see a crucial role for live, in-person training). Now for that sign.

The How-To Component of this Book

Event 1. I write section on the two purposes of this book (10:15-11:40 a.m.)

This you already know about. I was writing about the two purposes of this book: first, to let people know this phenomenon is there and is real; second, to teach people how to work with signs in their own lives. As you can see from that section, I continue to have many reservations about the second purpose, the how-to element.

Event 2. I read review of *The Journey That Never Was* (11:40 a.m.)

While writing that section, I had to reboot my computer, and while it was rebooting, I happened to pick up a *Course in Miracles* newsletter from my cluttered desk. I found reviews of two of my books, and then went on to read the next review, which was of a book titled *The Journey That Never Was* by DavidPaul and Candice Doyle.

According to this review, *The Journey That Never Was* is a book about listening to the Holy Spirit for guidance. It tells the authors' story of "hearing and sharing the Voice of the Holy Spirit, as a distinct and conversational voice, for over ten years." It also has a major how-to component: "Their book, *The Journey That Never Was*, weaves their personal experiences of hearing this Voice with practical, step-by-step exercises....It is a guide to hearing the Voice within you." What really struck me was the final paragraph, which seems to speak of two purposes for the book:

> If nothing else, their story is an inspiring one [purpose #1]. However, the authors believe that following their practical steps can empower you to receive guidance and support in every area of your life [purpose #2].

Throughout, then, the review implies that the book serves two purposes: first, it relates the authors' ten-year experience of following guidance and thus inspires readers (presumably with how real and helpful this phenomenon is); second, it teaches readers how to receive such guidance for their own lives.

Proximity (how close together in time the events were)

Simultaneous (the two events were no more than a minute apart)

Parallels (the elements both events share in common)

For simplicity's sake, I'll speak in terms of a single author, even though one of the books has two authors.

- A book on receiving guidance from a higher source (in the case of my book, what I called a "higher Planner"; in the case of the other book, the Holy Spirit)
- There is a statement about the purpose of the book.
- In this statement, two purposes are given for the book.

- One purpose is to impress on readers how real and important this way of receiving guidance is.
- The other is to teach them how to obtain such guidance themselves.
- The book includes copious examples from the author's many years of working with this kind of guidance.
- The author is a student and teacher of *A Course in Miracles.*

Notice that we are not dealing with just one parallel, but with a whole complex of them. We have a list of seven parallels, some of them quite specific, and all of them come together to form a whole picture.

Subject situation (the situation in one's life the sign is speaking to)

The subject situation is clearly my uncertainty about the how-to purpose of the book (although I think there is a secondary focus on the other purpose I gave for the book). I think that is intuitively obvious. However, as we will see in Chapter 5, there are also rules that point to this as the subject situation.

Interpretation (what the sign is saying about the subject situation)

What stands out is the fact that while I am so uncertain about the how-to component of this book, in the other book the how-to component is completely certain; indeed, it is front-and-center. I think one's gut instinct here is to see this as an answer to my uncertainty. You think, "Oh, he *is* supposed to have a how-to element in this book, just like that other book did." And that, as we'll see later, is exactly what the rules for interpretation would dictate. Here is my interpretation:

> My signs book should definitely include a how-to component. I can put my concerns to rest about that. On a larger level, it is right for the book to have the two purposes I have conceived of it having. It should both make people aware of the reality of signs and teach them how to work with signs. And it should support those purposes with copious examples of signs from my own life.

Though the latter part of the interpretation, about the "larger level," is important (and we'll see later how this dovetails with other signs about the book), the main focus of the sign is clearly the first sentence. The sign is confirming the rightness of having a how-to component in the book. It is telling me I can stop being anxious about that.

I will sometimes give CMPEs to my friend and colleague Greg Mackie to interpret independently. So I did that with this one. I gave him only two things. I gave him the review of *The Journey That Never Was* and I also gave him the above section titled "The purposes of this book." Greg, however, also needed to know my doubts about the how-to aspect of the book, since they are crucial background for the first event. However, if I had just told him of my doubts, that would have immediately flagged them as what the sign was about. So I took the paragraphs above in which I expressed those doubts (the second and third paragraphs of "A sign about the preceding section," beginning with the sentence "At first, I was adamant…") and wove them into the section "The purposes of this book." I made sure they appeared to be part of the original narrative, so as not to call Greg's attention to them.

Other than giving Greg the book review and an augmented version of the section "The purposes of this book," I said nothing to him, beyond telling him that both events occurred at the same time. Greg concluded that it was a CMPE and then offered this interpretation:

> Robert's decision to include material (in the signs book) on how to work with your own signs is correct. The material is useful and necessary, because all people want guidance for their own lives, and providing this is the very goal of signs.

You can see that Greg and I hit on exactly the same main point. I said, "This book should definitely include a how-to component." He said, "Robert's decision to include material (in the signs book) on how to work with your own signs is correct." We even gave similar titles to the sign. I called it "The How-To Component of this Book." He called it "Include the How-to Material."

Why is this so important? It means Greg and I are not just using the events of this sign as a kind of Rorschach inkblot onto which we project our own personal desires and expectations. It means, instead, that there is something *in the sign* that we are both independently seeing. The sign itself is expressing a particular perspective. It is speaking, not with my voice, not with Greg's voice, but with its *own* voice, a voice that two interpreters, working independently, can both hear.

Getting back to the CMPE itself, this is a perfect example. In terms of its structure, everything about it is typical. You have two independent events occurring very close together in time. These events share a whole complex of parallels between them. You have a subject situation that is personally relevant to me, the person the sign happened to. And you have the sign commenting on that subject situation in a way that resolves an uncertainty of mine.

What is also typical about this sign is the experience of being on the receiving end. I have had so many concerns about the how-to aspect of this book. I *had* decided to include it, but I would have had lingering doubts behind every sentence while writing it. To get a sign speaking to those very doubts is, quite frankly, a major relief. It says I can finally put my doubts to rest.

The relief, however, really goes beyond the specific answer, for the very fact that my question has been answered gives me a kind of concrete evidence that my needs are being looked out for. And in the end, the feeling that lends my life is a priceless additional blessing, over and above the value of any specific answers I may get along the way.

Since, as I mentioned, you too are involved in this sign, you may want to note your own experience of it. How do you feel about the how-to component of this book being affirmed? Does the sign seem to you to offer sound counsel? Does its counsel match your needs as a reader? Does it give you a feeling that someone or something is looking out for *your* needs?

Chapter 2
Entering the World of the Signs

The concept of signs or CMPEs (*Conjunctions of Meaningfully Parallel Events*) that I present in this book is one that developed very gradually for me. It was as if I were gazing into a deep lake for years, seeing some object rising slowly up out of the depths, so incredibly slowly that it took nearly thirty years from my first glimpse of a hazy, indistinct shape to seeing the object's actual contours as it finally surfaced.

My first glimpse of that hazy shape came when I was sixteen, on a night that ended up changing my life. The sign that occurred that night is perhaps not as amazing as some signs, yet it had a lasting impact on me. Besides changing my life and the lives of four other people, it is what started me down the path of working with signs.

King Kong

Since first grade, my best friend Kevin and I had done everything together. Yet in the last year or so I had begun to develop an avid inner life. I had been pondering big questions and developing my insights on paper, yet whenever I tried to share my thoughts and feelings with Kevin, he grew silent. As a result, I felt bottled up, alone. Another source of loneliness was the fact that I didn't have a girlfriend. I hadn't even been on a date.

I had no idea that all of this was about to suddenly change. For weeks I had looked forward to the release of the remake of the movie *King Kong*. On December 17, 1976, the movie was finally set to open. Naturally, I assumed Kevin would go with me. Yet when the night came, I was shocked when he told me he didn't feel like going. So I asked another friend—Darin—to go. I don't think Darin and I had ever done anything together outside of school, and as we sat in the theater before the movie started, talking away, it felt like a significant moment.

Without exchanging a word, Kevin and I never did another thing together. I am not really sure why. I guess we both just lost interest. We still lived three doors down from each other and belonged to the same circle of friends. But the friendship we had had for ten years came to an oddly abrupt and silent end.

After that night at *King Kong*, I started spending time with Darin. With Darin I finally had an outlet for all the thoughts that had been brewing inside me. We would regularly stay up past midnight talking about all the things I thought I couldn't talk about with anyone. It always struck me as significant that on a single night I lost my old best friend and gained a new one.

Yet this by itself doesn't constitute a CMPE. The other part of the story involves Susan, a girl I knew from my church youth group. She and her boyfriend Mike had been together for two years and expected to marry. It was, however, a volatile and conflict-ridden relationship. Susan felt stifled by Mike. Since childhood she had felt called to be a Lutheran pastor, but Mike informed her she would have to convert to his religion—Catholicism—in which, as a woman, she wouldn't be able to lead a church. He grew so possessive that he actually forbade her to say hello to her girlfriends at school.

In September of that year, however, Mike started college. Susan, still in high school, was left on her own and found herself enjoying a freedom she had really missed. Mike was set to be in Europe over Christmas vacation, and Susan used the opportunity to secretly plan a party, something she knew Mike wouldn't approve of. The party would take place at a friend's house on the evening of December 17, the same evening as my movie.

The night before the party, however, Mike told Susan his trip had fallen through. He would be around for the party! She quickly recovered and told him she was going to a party hosted by someone else. Her secret was safe for the time being, yet she had to ask herself, what sort of relationship would drive her to plan a party that her boyfriend couldn't attend and couldn't even know about? She thought about it all the next day, and when Mike showed up for the party, she did what she had to and broke off the relationship—right about the time my movie was starting.

Within a few weeks, Susan used her newfound freedom to ask me out. This began a relationship that would eventually lead to marriage and children. Between these two new relationships I felt as if I had a new life. I had a girlfriend I could share my feelings with and a best friend I could share my thoughts with. What always struck me as remarkable is that it all essentially happened on one night. At around 8 p.m. on December 17, both my and Susan's primary relationship came to an end, opening the way for new relationships to form between Susan and me, as well as Darin and me.

If I had understood then what I do now, I would have drawn up a list of parallels between my evening and Susan's evening. That list would have gone something like this:

- A teenager is in a long-time significant relationship, with either a best friend or a boyfriend.

- This teenager feels stifled in that relationship, unable to really express him- or herself (in my case, verbally; in Susan's case, behaviorally).

- The feeling of needing this expression has been getting more intense.

- The teen plans in advance a social event that is very important to him/her.

- In this event, it is important to the teen that the best friend or boyfriend play his assigned role, which is to either come or not come.

- Yet at the last minute, this person does just the opposite: doesn't come when he's supposed to or comes when he's not supposed to.

- This unexpected turn of events leads the teen to suddenly realize he or she doesn't want to be in this relationship.

- This leads to the end of the relationship.

- It also leads (either on that night or soon after) to the teen finding a new relationship, a new best friend or new boyfriend.

- I am in both new relationships: I find a new best friend and I *am* the new boyfriend.

This is a good list of parallels, perhaps the chief mark of a real CMPE. Not only are there a lot of them, but they come together to tell a single story. It is a story in which the tension within a certain relationship builds until a particular special occasion, when it breaks, ending the relationship and opening the way for new ones.

The events of that night left a deep impression on me. Due to an inexplicable confluence of events, I suddenly had a new life, in which I was no longer bottled up. I just knew this couldn't have been chance. It all seemed too meaningfully orchestrated. I had no idea what could have arranged events so intelligently, but I intuitively felt I had just glimpsed the workings of some invisible blueprint for my life. It was hard to shake the feeling that some power beyond the human had stepped in and set me free.

That night placed in my mind the notion that events could be arranged in meaningful ways and that these arrangements could reveal the intended outlines of my life. Over the next several years, these kinds of events continued to happen. A few of them were even as life-changing as the King Kong sign. Such occurrences left me with the feeling that some higher meaning had momentarily touched down in my life. When they happened, I would ponder their meaning, talk about them with friends, and fix their dates in my memory.

Ten years after the King Kong sign, a major turning point occurred in my relationship with signs. Susan and I had been married several years, and though we expected to have children, we had never seriously discussed it. Then on Christmas morning of 1986, we were opening presents at her brother's house and had to step out and buy some wine. While driving around looking for an open store, we discovered we had each that morning experienced a significant internal shift. Through totally different thought processes, we had each gotten past our own personal block to having a child. While struck with the coincidence and thinking something like "Oh my God, does this mean we are going to have a baby?" we drove past an ad on a bus stop that said, "Thinking of having a baby? Call 1-800-***-BABY"—the number of a local hospital's nursery. What made this ad hit even closer to home was that Susan's best friend was a nurse who worked in that very nursery and even at times manned that very hotline.

By the time the day was over, three other related events happened that seemed part of the sign, and all of them seemed to contain symbols of the child we would have, symbols that had a great deal in common with each other. All three symbols were men who shared several characteristics.

A little more than two years later, our first child was born, and true to the initial sign, it was indeed a boy, whom we named Adam. By this time I had started writing down some of the signs I experienced, but now it felt important to me to write down every sign about this child. The signs seemed to know so much about him—what parent wouldn't be intrigued by that?

So I began a journal in which I recorded the signs about my son. This is where my schooling in CMPEs began in earnest. I felt as if I were slowly being ushered into a fascinating and intricate world. I would take several pages to write about each sign, and over the course of those pages, patterns would emerge that I had no clue were there when I started writing. Fresh meanings and insights would emerge from out of the blue. I soon realized that each sign contained far more than what met the eye.

One of the main things I discovered is that the initial parallel that caught my attention was just the tip of the iceberg. Over and over again, I would find that first conspicuous parallel was surrounded by a host of other parallels that were less noticeable but no less present. For example, with the King Kong sign, what originally struck me was that on the same night, Susan and I had both experienced the end of a longstanding major relationship. It was only much later that I noticed all the other parallels that I listed above.

Along the way, a host of other rules gradually emerged. For instance, I slowly realized that the events need to be much closer together in time than I had originally assumed. At first, I had included "signs" whose events were separated from each other by days. What I eventually discovered, though, was that the really good ones tended to consist of events that were quite close together, usually within a few hours of each other, quite often simultaneous. Finally, I did the obvious thing and began to keep records of how far apart the events were. Before too many months had gone by, I saw that roughly half of signs had events within a half hour of each other. This frequency then fell rapidly until there were very few signs whose events were more than five hours apart, and no signs whose events were more than twelve. What resulted was a nice, smooth curve which vanished around the twelve-hour mark. Given that, how could I continue to include examples in which the events were even twenty-four hours apart, let alone several days apart?

I eventually began to write down all the signs that happened to me. Over the processing of literally hundreds of signs, my current four-point model, with its various sub-points, slowly came into view. I had begun by working by the seat of my pants, with no rules, just intuition and common sense. But I gradually saw there was a fairly simple structure to this phenomenon, a structure I saw repeated again and again and again.

As this structure came into view, I got far stricter in what I counted as a sign. In the beginning, I had counted virtually anything. To friends looking in from the outside, it often seemed a bit superstitious, and now that I look back on it, much of it looks that way to me, too. I eventually realized, though, that those occurrences that didn't fit the model were simply weaker all the way around, and thus much harder to distinguish from mere chance. I ultimately learned it was in my best interests to dispassionately set them aside.

Strangely, the more narrow and restrictive I got, the more amazing the signs got. It's as if I were throwing away the dross and leaving only the gold. The signs that remained had remarkable qualities. They seemed to have deep insight into the situations they spoke to, clearly deeper than that of the individuals involved. They even seemed to know the future. For instance, when my organization became involved in a copyright suit in 1999, the signs had already been speaking about this situation for eight years. Before I even knew the situation would exist, they had accurately forecast the basic story that would unfold over the next dozen or so years (I'll tell this story in full in Chapter 8).

Perhaps the single most arresting thing I observed was the astonishing consistency among signs. Different signs would revisit the same situations, say extremely similar things about them, use some of the same symbols, and even occur on the same dates in different years. Many times I had the experience of writing up a particular sign and then looking through my files for related signs, only to discover that years before a similar one had occurred on the exact same date. That still happens regularly, yet it never ceases to amaze me.

For most of my history with signs, I have worked with them by myself. Yet in the mid- to late-90's a few people around me began to take personal interest in the signs. Signs were happening to them, and they wanted my help with interpreting them. A couple of people went even further and wanted to learn how to interpret signs themselves. Greg Mackie is a fellow teacher at the Circle of Atonement. Not long after he arrived in Sedona in 1997 to train to teach with the Circle, signs started to come about his future function as a Course teacher and scholar, and I shared these with him. He immediately grasped the concept and was hooked. Greg has one of those disciplined minds that is completely at home in hewing to a set of intellectual rules. He quickly caught on to the rules in this case and has been working with signs ever since.

Nicola is my second wife. She and I met in England in 1999 and began corresponding. Not long after, I gave her a lengthy introduction to my concept of signs (which was itself the occasion of a sign, one I will share in the last chapter). Like Greg, Nicola soon began having her own signs, and like Greg, she took to the concept instantly. She intuitively recognized that here was a real phenomenon in its own right, one with its own rules. She soon became quite adept at working with signs herself.

What neither Nicola nor I realized was that, by meeting, we had embarked on a journey that would lead to the two of us setting out on a new life together. What we also didn't realize was the role that signs would play in this journey. To a large degree, they guided us through it, as our former marriages dissolved, Nicola moved to America, and we worked to build a new life and family here. At each point along the way, a sign would be there giving us needed guidance on which way to go. We depended on them, and they responded by displaying what seemed like a remarkable ability to help us navigate through a very complex situation.

My relationship with the CMPEs is very much an evolving one. Just as we take years, even decades, to really get to know the people in our lives, so it has taken me these thirty years to get to know the "voice" of the signs, and I am still getting to know it. What have I learned about this voice? Answering that, of course, is the purpose of this book. Yet for now I can boil it down to two things.

First, my experience has taught me that this voice is for real. This is not a case of me imaginatively connecting dots that are in truth unrelated. There is an intelligence animating these events. As infants, we quickly learn there is intelligence guiding the behavior of the bodies moving around us. We thus end up relating to those bodies totally differently than we relate to things that move randomly, such as the trees swaying in the wind. After watching the "behavior" of signs for all these years, I am no longer capable of treating them like trees swaying randomly in the wind (even though that's how I have come to see much of synchronicity). I literally cannot bring myself to doubt there is an intelligence behind them, any more than I can doubt there is an intelligence behind the behavior of the human bodies around me.

Second, I have learned to trust this voice. Imagine there is someone in your life who, when she speaks, speaks with wisdom far exceeding that of other people you know. She sees so deeply into things that her insights regularly expand your mind. Her comments even betray an uncanny awareness of the future. She also appears to be completely unbiased; her views seem truly fair to all concerned. And while other people flip-flop back and forth, she never wavers. After years of being around her, she would have your trust. It's as simple as that. Whatever you thought about where she got her insight, you would be unable to *withhold* your trust from her. This is exactly my experience with the signs. They have done more than earn my trust; they have *compelled* my trust. Which is why, for some time now, my life has been in their hands.

Chapter 3
Events

Krusty the Father

I was taking my thirteen-year-old son Adam to the football field at the local high school to throw the Frisbee around. Here in the desert, it's a treat just to have some nice green grass to run around on. I had always loved taking the kids to play outdoors, but it had been months since I had done so. My first wife and I were at that time involved in a lengthy and intense process of evaluating whether our marriage would continue, and I had allowed my focus to wander from the kids. So as I drove to the high school, I was feeling guilty, but also like I was coming back to a central priority. I remember thinking there might well be a sign around this.

We got onto the football field and started throwing the Frisbee. After we had been at it a while, Adam got a bit lazy and just laid down in the grass on his back. I turned this into a game by seeing if I could get the Frisbee to actually land on him. It eventually got too dark and, after a nice time, we went home.

Later that evening, I watched an episode of *The Simpsons* (titled "Insane Clown Poppy"). In it, Krusty the Clown (everyone's nightmare combination of children's entertainer and disgusting old man) discovers he has a daughter. Even though he has been entertaining kids his whole life, he doesn't know the first thing about them. He has absolutely no clue how to be a father. His newfound daughter begs him to spend time with her and finally convinces him to take her to the beach. There, she wants to play Frisbee, but he is too lazy and lays down on his back on the beach towel, asking her to throw it so that it hits him while he lays there. Realizing what a rotten father he is, he watches Homer play with his kids. He ends up asking Homer (of all people!) to be his mentor in being a good father.

The image of the girl throwing the Frisbee at Krusty while he's lying down jolted me to attention. I had just lived through an uncannily similar scene. I knew this had to be a sign. It didn't take long to discover a host of parallels surrounding that first one:

- A father hasn't been spending time with his child or children.
- Father and child go on a special outing to a park or beach.
- This trip is either a first for them or is the first time in a long time.
- There, they play Frisbee.
- But one of them is too lazy and lays down on his back.
- The game then turns into the other person throwing the Frisbee so that it will hit the one on the ground.
- While on this outing, the father feels inadequate as a father.
- He decides he will be a better father.

This sign is so clear and straightforward that, once you read the parallels, it needs no further interpretation. It was clearly backing up my recognition that I hadn't been spending enough time with my kids and my decision to change that. But it did so in such a stinging way. Being likened to a degenerate clown, who first didn't know he was a father and then discovers he is a terrible father, was not exactly an inspirational moment. In fact, Nicola at one point urged me to stop telling people this sign, feeling that it simply wasn't a balanced snapshot of me as a father.

The fact is, however, that it's a great example of how signs work. They often present a caricature of things, and probably for the same reason that we caricature things. It makes a point, and does so in an unforgettable way. After that, it's up to us to take away a proportional message from the caricature, one that neither overshoots nor underplays its intended meaning. When you see, for instance, an artistic caricature that has a gigantic nose, you know that person's nose is not that big in real life. But you also know it's not petite and perfect.

In this chapter, we will begin exploring my four-point model of CMPEs (*Conjunctions of Meaningfully Parallel Events*). The first point is *events*. To qualify as a CMPE, an occurrence must include:

- at least two distinct events;
- that are "independent";
- that occurred in close proximity—within hours of each other; and
- that are strikingly similar.

If you are a believer in synchronicity, you will find this model is almost certainly tighter than what you are used to. Therefore, with each of the above four sub-points, I will try to explain the reason for it being so tight. I am not implying that things that fall outside these specific parameters are necessarily the product of random chance. It's just so much harder to be confident that they aren't.

At least two distinct events

To have a real CMPE, you need at least two distinct events that occur together in time. There can be more than two, but there *cannot* be less. A "one-event CMPE" is another way of saying "not a CMPE."

This simple rule is surprisingly easy to forget. The reason, I believe, is that we are so used to thinking about a "sign" as being a single unusual event that (to our eyes) is clearly speaking to some situation of ours. This event probably occurs somewhere in the midst of an ongoing situation in our lives, and somehow we "know" that it's connected to that situation.

But how do we know? Let's say, for instance, I've been wrestling with insomnia. After a year of this, I happen to pick up a hitchhiker one day, and this man, without any prompting from me, tells me he has insomnia but has found this amazing herbal remedy for it. I could easily take this as a "sign" that I should use the same remedy. But can I really be confident that my conversation with him and my insomnia are connected? After all, over the course of my year with insomnia, I've had 365 days to run into someone who also has insomnia and seems to have a cure. The odds of this happening purely by chance, then, are pretty good, too good to overlook.

These odds get dramatically reduced, however, when we require that there be two distinct events *on the same day*. Let's say, for instance, that just before picking up this hitchhiker, I had been to the health food store, where a clerk told me about his insomnia and recommended the same herbal remedy. Now we have two events right next to each other. Who wouldn't find this second scenario more remarkable?

I say "*at least* two distinct events" because many CMPEs (about one-third by my records) have three or more events. These are what I call "multiple-event signs" ("multiple" in this case referring to more than two). Most are three- and four-event signs, but occasionally I'll have signs with five, six, seven, or even eight events. These can be incredibly impressive. Imagine eight events occurring on one day that are all strikingly similar, and yet no visible cause brought them together. When you actually witness such a thing, it knocks your socks off.

For simplicity's sake, however, I'll be referring to multiple-event signs only occasionally in this book. In general, I will confine our discussion to two-event signs.

Independent

What I mean by "independent" is *causally* independent. In other words, two such similar events occurred together not because one event influenced the other, or because both were caused by a third event or condition. Rather, these two events *just happened* to be this parallel and come together this closely in time. To all appearances, they were causally independent, leaving us without a good conventional explanation for why two such parallel things happened to land right next to each other.

Independence is crucial. Without it, you don't have anything synchronistic at all. Rather, you have the normal course of things. We humans cause similar events to happen together all the time. Imagine, for instance, that playing Frisbee with my son reminded me of an episode of *The Simpsons* in which Krusty plays a comparable game of Frisbee with his daughter, and then I went home and pulled that episode from my video collection and watched it. No one would attribute anything mystical or synchronistic to that. It's just human behavior.

When you have a potential CMPE, therefore, it's crucial to look at this issue carefully and honestly. A lot of potential CMPEs fail on the testing ground of independence. You look at the events more closely, for instance, and realize the second event was somehow influenced by the first. Indeed, that is the main thing to look out for—one event being *under the influence* of the other.

As crucial as independence is, it is often not black or white. There are definite gray areas. For example, in our office at the Circle of Atonement, Nicola told Alexandra, our office manager, that she was e-mailing her an article critiquing the DVD *The Secret*. While Alexandra was downloading her e-mail to get it, she right then received another e-mail about *The Secret*, asking for *our* critique of it. This seemed pretty remarkable, until you realize that at that time *The Secret* was everywhere. It had just been on *Oprah*, it was #1 on Amazon.com, and as a result, we were receiving e-mails about it all the time. I myself was e-mailed two articles about it that day.

Questionable independence like this does not necessarily rule out a CMPE. What it does, though, is put a great deal of pressure on the other factors to be especially strong. In this case, for instance, you would want a really excellent list of parallels. Yet, in fact, there is only one: an e-mail from someone critiquing *The Secret* or asking for a critique of it. As we'll see in the next chapter, one parallel is not enough.

The main thing is to honestly examine the issue of independence. Ask yourself, "Are there normal sorts of cause and effect that could reasonably account for these two events being this similar and this close in time?" The more strongly you answer "yes," the more you disqualify these events from being a CMPE.

In close proximity

The two events *have* to be close together in time. This is absolutely essential and should be one of the very first things you look at. In tracking the proximity between events for signs over a three-year period, I found the following:

- In 55% of signs, the events were within thirty minutes of each other.
- In 90%, the events were within five hours of each other.
- In 100%, the events were within twelve hours of each other.

Based on this, when I evaluate a potential sign, I consider it *strengthened* if the events were within a half hour of each other, *weakened* if they were more than five hours apart, and *disqualified* if they were more than twelve hours apart.

In my experience, this issue of proximity is one where you will be greatly tempted to stretch the rules. "The events were only two days apart. Doesn't that qualify?" However, it is in your interests to be rigorous with proximity. The wider you cast the net in terms of time, the less confidence you can have that you are dealing with anything other than the normal workings of probability. If you let enough time pass, eventually a second event will almost certainly come along that is remarkably similar to the first. That's just probability. And if you take it as some sort of sign from the heavens, then you are reading mystical significance into the meaningless patterns of probability. Is that what you really want?

Strikingly similar

Finally, the two events, of course, need to be strikingly similar. In a real CMPE, you are struck by how incredibly parallel the two events are. You generally begin by noticing a particular parallel between them, and then, the more you look, the more parallels come into view.

I won't say much about this characteristic here, since it will be the topic of the next chapter. For now, what is important to know is that we are talking about actual, objective similarity. This is distinctly different from the more subjective relationship we often see between supposedly synchronistic events.

As an example of the latter, an author on coincidence relates the story of a first date in Manhattan. He and his date visit a small park and enjoy an intimate dinner. After a pleasant evening, he returns to his car to find that someone has broken into it and stolen his tape deck and tapes. He wonders if this isn't a symbolic warning, cautioning him that this relationship will end up taking away "the psychological capacity to *play the music*—to fully enjoy myself in a lighthearted way."[9]

Notice, however, that there is no objective connection between the date and the theft. He just *sees* a connection between them. He sees the theft as providing the answer to how this relationship will turn out. This is perhaps the norm with synchronicity. We see one event as the question (or the problem, or the need) and the other as the answer. Yet we can easily imagine that the line we draw to connect these dots is purely in our heads. Look at the steps our man went through in his thinking: 1) this theft has symbolic meaning; 2) that meaning applies to this new relationship (rather than some other situation); 3) it means the relationship will take away his lightheartedness. With each one of these steps, notice how easy it is to entertain the idea that it is purely his imagination. As an outsider, it is hard to see a compelling reason to draw his conclusions.

That is why we want an objective similarity between the two events. This means they are connected in a way that anyone can see. Otherwise, you don't know if they are connected at all, apart from in your imagination.

Examples

We will see examples throughout this book that satsify all of the above qualifications. Therefore, I'll provide just a couple of brief ones here.

Let's first look at the familiar example of Jung's scarab. While a patient is telling Jung her dream of being given a golden scarab piece of jewelry, Jung notices that an actual gold-green scarab beetle is tapping at the window. He opens the window, catches it in mid-air, and hands it to his patient, saying, "Here is your scarab."

Now let's run this through the above requirements:

1. *Were there at least two distinct events (rather than one event occurring alongside an ongoing situation)?*
   Yes. Event 1 was the patient telling her dream. Event 2 was the scarab beetle showing up.
2. *Were the events independent, so that their similarity and proximity were*

seemingly a product of chance, rather than a product of one event being influenced by the other, or both events being influenced by a third event?

Yes, it is hard to see how the telling of the dream could have in any way caused the appearance of the beetle. Jung opening the window, catching the beetle, and giving it to his patient was obviously a product of her telling her dream. But the initial appearance of the beetle at the window was not, at least not by any normal account of causation.

3. *Were the events within twelve hours of each other? (The potential sign is strengthened if they were within a half hour and weakened if they were more than five hours apart.)*

Yes, they were simultaneous, so the potential sign is strengthened.

4. *Were the events strikingly similar, sharing an objective similarity rather than a merely subjective, imaginative connection?*

Yes, both events contained a golden scarab.

As you can see, Jung's scarab story passes these tests with flying colors. Unfortunately, as we have seen, it ultimately fails as a CMPE, but that is a matter of not enough parallels, which is the subject of our next chapter. In terms of the requirements of *this* chapter, it is a model example.

Another example: One morning I was reading a new book to my two-year-old daughter Miranda, a book from the 1940's that I had never heard of. She had recently been given it by a friend of ours who loves reading stories to children and who wrote in the card that she wished she could read this one to Miranda. The book, *Blueberries for Sal*, tells the story of a little girl named Sal. She and her mother take pails and drive to Blueberry Hill to pick blueberries. There, they have a bit of an adventure: They encounter a large bear and her cub, though they escape unharmed.

About eight hours later, I sat down with Miranda again, this time to watch a TV show. Nicola was concerned that, in the wake of her little brother's birth, Miranda was taking in too much TV. She had heard that *Dora the Explorer* was good for kids, especially because it was an interactive experience, not a passive one. She therefore recorded an initial episode of it for Miranda, and this is what Miranda and I were sitting down to watch. In it, Dora goes on an adventure with her monkey friend. They take a pail and travel to Blueberry Hill to pick blueberries. There they encounter a large bear but ultimately escape unharmed. I wondered if this might be a sign.

Let's run this example through our requirements:

1. *Were there at least two distinct events (rather than one event occurring alongside an ongoing situation)?*
   Yes. Event 1 was me reading *Blueberries for Sal* to Miranda. Event 2 was me watching *Dora the Explorer* with Miranda.
2. *Were the events independent, so that their similarity and proximity were seemingly a product of chance, rather than a product of one event being influenced by the other, or both events being influenced by a third event?*
   Yes, I had no idea the *Dora* episode would be so similar to *Blueberries for Sal*. The independence is very slightly weakened in that having a two-year-old means that a lot of children's stories pass our way. So the likelihood of encountering two similar stories on a given day is greater for us than for others. But this slightly weakened independence is more than offset by the impressive similarity we'll see below.
3. *Were the events within twelve hours of each other? (The potential sign is strengthened if they were within a half hour and weakened if they were more than five hours apart.)*
   Yes, but they were more than five hours apart, so the potential sign is weakened.
4. *Were the events strikingly similar, sharing an objective similarity rather than a merely subjective, imaginative connection?*
   Yes, both events shared a long list of similarites. Robert and Miranda take in a children's story together. It is new for Miranda, having been "given" her by a woman (Nicola or our friend) who expressly wants Miranda to have an interactive experience with it (interactive TV or being read to). This story involves a little girl and a companion going on an adventure. They take a pail or pails with them. They go to Blueberry Hill to pick blueberries. There, they encounter a large bear but escape from this encounter unharmed.

As you can see, this example also passes the tests. It is very slightly weak on independence and weak on proximity, but that weakness is compensated for by the amazingly strong similarities between the events. In contrast to the one parallel of Jung's scarab, here we have an integrated complex of them. This is a real CMPE.

Starting a sign journal, evaluating the events

If you are going to notice and work with your own CMPEs, I strongly suggest you keep a written journal. Have a notebook or a place on your computer where you record and process potential CMPEs.

Once you have a sign journal, what do you do? Do you somehow prepare yourself to have CMPEs? Do you do something to draw them into your life? Do you ask questions that they will answer? My answer to all these questions is generally "no." I'm not all that convinced that anything we specifically do to elicit CMPEs has much, if any, effect. They are responsive, yes, but in my experience, your *life* is the question that they respond to. They don't seem particularly responsive to explicit questions (though, to be quite honest, it is hard to tell).

So once you have that journal for recording them, just keep your eyes peeled. Stay vigilant. What you want to look for is any case in which you find yourself saying, "Huh. That was weird," any case in which you notice an odd similarity between two events that are close together in time.

As I said in the first chapter, the key is to not allow that "huh" reaction to pass you by. When you experience it, stop and then begin evaluating the potential CMPE according to the model.

The first step is to evaluate the events to see if they meet the criteria outlined in this chapter. To do that, take the potential CMPE through the flow chart below and see how it fares. Be aware that at this point, you are not attempting to reach a definite conclusion about whether something is or isn't a sign. You are just trying to see if it passes the first hurdle. (The remaining hurdles will be explored in the following chapters.)

In fact, if you have a potential CMPE, then, you might try taking it through this flow chart now:

Were there at least two distinct events (rather than one event occurring alongside an ongoing situation)?	If yes, move to next question.	If no, stop here. It's not a sign
Were the events independent, so that their similarity and proximity were seemingly a product of chance , rather than a product of one event being influenced by the other, or both events being influenced by a third event?	If yes, move to next question.	If no, stop here. It's not a sign
Were the events within twelve hours of each other? (The potential sign is strengthened if they were within a half hour and weakened if they were more than five hours apart.	If yes, move to next question.	If no, stop here. It's not a sign
Were the events strikingly similar, sharing an objective similarity rather than a merely subjective, imaginative connection?	If yes, and you've made it this far, it may be a sign.	If no, stop here. It's not a sign

If the potential sign passes the above tests, now would be a good time to write a fairly complete account of both events. This will be essential for the steps to come.

Once the events are written down, move through your potential CMPE, step by step, according to the material in the following three chapters. First, write down and evaluate the parallels, according to the instructions in Chapter 4. If the parallels appear to meet the requisite criteria, go on and identify the subject situation, according to the instructions in Chapter 5. Finally, try your hand at an interpretation, according to the instructions in Chapter 6.

To clarify how to do all this, the ends of Chapter 4 and 6 contain exercises that lead you through identifying the parallels, subject situation, and interpretation of sample signs.

Chapter 4
Parallels

Family Comes First

It was New Year's Eve. Nicola and I, our sixteen-month old daughter Miranda, and Nicola's parents, Mick and Pauline, had been invited to spend time at a friend's house in Hawaii. Nicola and I were relaxing after a very intense year. On the weekdays, I had spent hours each day writing for a study program on *A Course in Miracles*, and on weekends I worked on the book you are reading. This left me with little time each day to take Miranda off Nicola's hands so she could get her own work done, let alone rest. She was wiped out, and so was I.

That morning, she and I took a walk along the beautiful beach nearby and talked about the year to come. Nicola frankly didn't have much enthusiasm. She assumed next year would be more of the same. I assured her that without the Course study program (which was ending that day), I would be able to devote much more time to the family. In fact, since we had arrived in Hawaii, I had been trying to show her that things would be different by taking Miranda most of each day, allowing Nicola to relax on the beach or hang out with her parents. During our walk, we also devised a new plan for the weekends. Since this book was almost done (or so we thought), instead of writing, I would take Miranda on Saturday and we would have family time on Sunday. With these understandings in place, I think we both breathed a sigh of relief about the new year. The past year just hadn't felt balanced.

That evening, I was sitting with Nicola's parents in front of our friend's wide screen TV. Actually, I was on my knees on the floor, trying to get the volume to work. I had wrestled with the six clickers (!) already. Now I had the cabinet open and was fiddling with one of six pieces of mysterious hardware, with no success. Then Miranda, who was barely beginning to walk, toddled over, opened the other side of the cabinet, and began randomly pushing buttons on another one of those six units. To my utter shock, a volume bar appeared across the bottom of the TV screen. She had actually fixed the sound problem! Nicola's mum Pauline and I were flabbergasted. My one-year-old had succeeded where I had failed. We just howled with laughter.

A little later in the evening, Nicola had joined us and we were all getting ready to watch *Click*, a movie starring Adam Sandler. And there I was, fiddling with the volume again. Miranda had solved the problem for TV shows, but not for DVDs. As she was in bed, I had to solve it on my own, which I actually managed to do just as the opening scene popped on the screen.

That opening scene felt like déjà vu. We see a coffee table with four different remote controls on it. Sandler wants to turn on the TV, but he can't figure out which remote is which. As he fumbles with them, instead of turning on the TV, he opens the garage door, turns on the fan, and starts a toy car. Then his little five-year-old daughter adroitly picks up the correct remote and instantly turns on the TV. Pauline and I looked at each other with an unspoken "What?" This was ridiculously similar to what Miranda had done.

Another strange thing happened during the movie. The story takes place on a fourth of July weekend, on which the entire family (including Sandler's parents) is supposed to go on a family camping trip. On the first evening, the family is having a picnic while fireworks are going off everywhere. Some kids nearby keep setting off loud firecrackers, disrupting the family picnic and causing Sandler to yell at them and finally chase them off.

While watching the movie, we (who of course were on our own family vacation over a holiday) found ourselves surrounded by the sound of fireworks. In terms of fireworks, New Year's Eve in Hawaii put to shame any Fourth of July I had ever experienced. Indeed, for what must have been a solid half hour, the people next door were setting off strings of firecrackers literally a few feet outside our windows. We could barely hear the movie. I couldn't exactly yell at them and chase them off, so I settled for closing every window I could find.

What was most striking of all, however, was the movie itself, which was really a morality play. It was all about an overworked man who keeps prioritizing his work over his family. His wife is deeply distressed and demoralized by this, and he keeps promising it will change. We watch, however, as he continues to choose (aided by a "universal" remote-control he acquired after the opening scene) to prioritize work and avoid family. This plays out over the course of a lifetime, until he at last realizes the folly of his choices, and surrounded by his family, utters what seem to be his dying words: "Family comes first!"

This is what I call a four-event sign. There was the talk with Nicola in the morning (event 1), me trying to get the TV to work properly (event 2), the movie *Click* (event 3), and the fireworks going off outside the window (event 4). Among these four events, there was a solid list of parallels:

- A father is trying (and failing) to get the TV to work with multiple clickers (events 2, 3).

- His very young daughter does it instead in next to no time (2, 3).

- The father's work is significantly cutting into his family time (1, 3).

- His wife is especially concerned about and demoralized by this (1, 3).

- The father is promising this will change (1, 3).

- There is an important family vacation, which faces the father with a chance to prioritize the family (1, 3—I didn't explain this part about the movie, but it was there).

- Either the mother's or father's parents come along on the family vacation (1, 3).

- The vacation takes place over a major holiday, one that is associated with fireworks (New Year's—1, 4—or Fourth of July—3).

- At the holiday celebration, while the family is spending time together in the evening, someone sets off firecrackers (3, 4).

- This creates an annoyance for the family, which the father deals with (3, 4).

The message in this sign was not particularly subtle. Even without me going through the interpretation process, you can probably sense it. The meat of it is really in my discussion with Nicola in the morning (event 1) and *Click* (event 3), both of which had the same main point. The sign was affirming what Nicola and I had decided that morning, that I needed to decrease my work time and spend more time with the family. Indeed, notice how the bulk of the parallels depict me not at work, but on a holiday with my family. The message couldn't be clearer. I needed to put into practice the lesson of the movie: "Family comes first."

We will now explore the second point in our four-point model: *parallels*. Once you are satisfied that you have two discrete, independent events that are close in time and seem strikingly similar, the next step is to carefully explore just *how* similar they are. This means making a list of the parallels—the items that show up in both events.

The parallels are central to the whole CMPE process. More than anything else, they are what distinguish CMPEs (*Conjunctions of Meaningfully Parallel Events*) from the more usual sorts of synchronicity. They are also the main test of whether or not you have an actual CMPE. Furthermore, they usually drive much or all of the interpretation. *Everything* hinges on them.

As I mentioned in the previous chapter, these parallels need to be features that are genuinely shared by both events. They need to be objective similarities between the two events, ones that everyone could agree on. They cannot be the more imaginative kind of connection we often draw: "And when my friend said that, I just knew it was the answer to my dilemma."

To find all of the parallels in a potential sign, you need to gather as much information as you can about the events. If you were not present for all of an event, then do what you can to find out about the whole thing. If, for instance, one of the events was you watching part of a movie, try to get a hold of the movie and watch all of it. If you were directly present for the entire event, then write down your recollection of it as soon as possible and then have that recollection checked and filled out by someone else who was present. It will help to actually write the events down, in detail. You need to be working from accounts that are as complete and accurate as possible.

A strong list of parallels will have the following features:

- One or more specific, unlikely parallels
- A number of additional, more general parallels
- The list of parallels describes a general situation.
- The list captures something central about each event.

If you have a list of parallels with all these features, the list will almost certainly strike you—or anyone—as incredibly improbable. And that is what you need. If you look at the list of parallels from the opening story in this chapter, that will give you a flavor of what a good list of parallels looks like.

1. One or more specific, unlikely parallels

This is how the noticing of a CMPE begins. You observe a remarkable parallel between two events, a parallel that has no conventional reason to be there. With the bucket brigade sign (Chapter 1), for instance, we thought, "Hey, we just formed a bucket brigade, right after we talked about doing exactly that." With "Krusty the Father" (Chapter 3) I thought, "That odd game of Frisbee they are playing looks exactly like the one I just played." Or with the sign that opens this chapter, Pauline and I spontaneously looked at each other with "What?" clearly written on both our faces.

This is how it starts. As I said in Chapter 1, the crucial thing is to not stop here, but to instead keep looking for more parallels. Indeed, once you have satisfied yourself that the events pass the tests we covered in the last chapter (two distinct events, independent, in close proximity, and strikingly similar), the best thing to do is to make a list of parallels. Often, it is not until I get that list on paper that I really know whether I have a CMPE or not.

In making the list, there are two things you should remember. First, you need to word each parallel in such a way that it reflects both events. Once you have written the parallel down, look back and forth at the two events and make sure your wording fits them both.

For instance, in "Family Comes First," the first parallel I have is "A father is trying (and failing) to get the TV to work with multiple clickers." This is my attempt to describe two slightly different events. In my situation, the father was trying to get the TV volume to work using six clickers. In the movie, the father was trying to get the TV to *turn on* using *four*. If you look at the wording I chose, you can see that it fits both events equally well.

Second, I find it best to break the parallels into their smallest reasonable units. Try not to have parallels that are composed of several elements. For example, in "Family Comes First," I could have combined the first two parallels to make one larger one: "A father is trying (and failing) to get the TV to work with multiple clickers. His very young daughter does it instead in next to no time." However, I think it is better to list this as two separate parallels. First, it is easy to see it as two. You can easily imagine the father's struggle all by itself, without the daughter's part ever happening. Each part, in other words, is able to stand on its own. Second, breaking the parallels into their smallest reasonable units will enable you to count them, and this will help you decide if you have a genuine sign. How you break them into the smallest reasonable units is a pretty subjective affair, and different people do it somewhat differently. But it still helps to break them up for the sake of counting.

2. A number of additional, more general parallels

That first striking parallel, however, is not enough. In a real CMPE, you will find a number of others. This, in fact, is where the wheat gets separated from the chaff. A number of potential signs quickly fail at this very point.

For example, Nicola and I recently had a baby, a boy named Michael. One evening we were trying desperately—and unsuccessfully—to console him, just as we had on so many previous nights. We finally put it together: the inconsolable crying at the same time each day—he must have colic. About two minutes later on a game show that Nicola was watching, the correct answer to one of the questions was "colic." We looked at each other, but then quickly ran through our heads that there was only one parallel, and shrugged it off. A real sign would have many more parallels surrounding that first one.

This is also where Jung's scarab story failed. It had a spectactularly specific and unlikely parallel: a golden scarab. But that was it. Actually, to be perfectly fair, we cannot be entirely sure that was it. I think there is a slight chance that if we knew the details of the woman's dream and the details of that particular session with Jung, we would find a host of parallels between them. This underscores the great need to keep looking for more parallels based on a detailed account of both events.

Perhaps most potential CMPEs are like my colic example—just one parallel. But every now and then, you discover that right around that first parallel are a whole list of other ones. That first specific parallel, it turns out, is set within a whole parallel context. It is remarkable when you see it. That is the moment when I know I have a CMPE.

"Krusty the Father" is a perfect example. To refresh your mind about the story, I go to the local high school to play Frisbee with my son. Because this is our first outing in a long time, I feel guilty but also determined to get back to doing more with my children. My son gets lazy and ends up laying on the grass, leaving me to try to get the Frisbee to land on him. Later that evening, I watch an episode of *The Simpsons* in which Krusty the Clown discovers he has a daughter. She begs him to take her to the beach. They play Frisbee, but he is too lazy and he lays down, so the game becomes her trying to hit him with the Frisbee. He realizes he has no idea how to be a father and asks Homer to be his mentor.

The first parallel you notice, of course, is the unconventional Frisbee game, with one person lying down out of laziness and the other throwing the Frisbee so that it will hit him. But then you start noticing that this one specific parallel is embedded within a whole parallel context. It's not just any two people playing Frisbee. It's a father and child. This father hasn't been spending time with his child. Therefore, he takes the child on a special outing, which is either the first one or the first one in a long time. While on this outing, he feels inadequate as a father. He decides that he will be a better father.

There is no conventional reason why that parallel Frisbee game should be planted within this entire parallel context. It is much easier to imagine it standing by itself. The fact that it's not is what makes the whole thing so difficult to explain. How can two events come together purely by chance yet have this much in common?

What you need, then, is not one parallel but a *list* of parallels. This list will be a mix of specific, unlikely parallels surrounded by more general parallels. How long should the list be? My lists average about eight parallels (the CMPE that opens this chapter has a list of ten). When I start getting below five or six, I start worrying that I have nothing there. At that point, that list better contain some *very* specific and unlikely parallels, or else it is probably not a sign.

3. The list of parallels describes a general situation

A good list of parallels will never be a diverse laundry list of unrelated items. Rather, the items will come together to describe a general situation, with the specific parallels being the foreground of that situation and the general parallels being the background.

In fact, most lists of parallels tell a clear *story*. If you go back to the signs that begin Chapters 2 and 3 ("King Kong" and "Krusty the Father") and look at the lists of parallels there, you will see immediately that they tell a story.

The parallels describe a single situation because, in each event, you have the same basic pieces fitting together in the same basic way. You have, in other words, the same constellation showing up intact in two different events.

For instance, if you look at the list of parallels for "Family Comes First" (beginning of this chapter), you see a number of parts: a father, a daughter, a wife, parents (of the father or wife), clickers, a family vacation, firecrackers, the father's job, prioritizing the family. However, what is really remarkable about this list of common elements is that they fit together in the same way in both the movie and the real-life events: The *father* fails to get the *clickers* to work, while his *daughter* succeeds. The *father's work* is causing him to not *prioritize the family*, which is demoralizing his *wife*. The *family vacation*, on which the *parents* go as well, is a chance for the father to *prioritize the family*. On the *family vacation*, someone disrupts the family gathering with loud *firecrackers*, and the *father* has to deal with the disruption.

In other words, you don't just have a scattered pile of parts that happen to appear in independent events. Rather, in each event you not only have the same basic parts, but these parts are *assembled in roughly the same way*. This results in an overall constellation that is shared by both events. This is why the list of parallels tells a single story, because both events contain the same essential story. And seeing this shared story—seeing the same basic elements connected in the same basic ways—greatly increases our confidence that the two events are genuinely linked.

When you make a list of parallels, it is helpful to arrange them in a logical order that captures their unity. Try to arrange them in a way that best tells the story. You'll see how I've tried to do that in our various examples.

4. The list captures something central about each event

At least part of the reason a good list of parallels is unified is that it captures something central about the two events. The list will contain some peripheral elements, but its broad strokes will be made up of central elements. As a result, the list as a whole will tap into the heart of each event.

You can see this with all the signs I have related so far. For instance, in "Family Comes First" (beginning of this chapter), the parallels paint the following picture: The father's work is compromising his time with the family and he faces the choice between the two in relation to a particular family vacation. This goes to the heart of the movie *Click* and also to the heart of my conversation with Nicola earlier that day. Those two events, in other words, had not just overlapped; they had overlapped at their core.

One side benefit of this is that a good list of parallels will often cause you to understand the real essence of each event much better. You will see more deeply into its soul, so to speak. You will grasp its central dynamics in a way you didn't before.

In my mind, the fact that CMPEs are composed of events that join at their center strengthens the impression that the events really are connected, that it's not just our imagination. If the two events shared only a smattering of peripheral similarities, we would have more reason to wonder if we were trying to connect dots that weren't actually connected.

The improbability of the list as a whole

When you look at a list that has all four of the above characteristics, what immediately hits you is just how improbable it is. It seems absurdly beyond chance that two events could just happen to bump into each other and share a list of parallels like this—a list that contains some very specific and unlikely parallels, a list that includes so many parallels, a list that comes together to describe a general situation, and a list that captures so much of the heart of both events. It strains the mind to think this was all due to chance. The mind is involuntarily pushed into imagining that something more than chance was at work here.

It would be great if we could somehow quantify the probabilities involved—plug various factors into an equation and come up with a number—but, unfortunately, I don't think there is any way of doing that. The things we are dealing with, I believe, are just too impossibly complex. How, for instance, do you figure out the probability of a father unsuccessfully fumbling with multiple remotes, only to have his small daughter succeed? I have no idea. Yet figuring that out is just the barest beginning of assigning numerical probabilities to a sign like "Family Comes First."

I think we will have to rely on an intuitive reading to determine if a certain list of parallels is improbable enough. Such a "probability sniff test" will necessarily be subjective, yet I still think it can be quite adequate to the task. First, it can be honed and seasoned by contact with CMPEs. The more of them you encounter, the more you learn what a real one looks like. Second, solid signs are so wildly improbable that virtually anyone can admit that something truly extraordinary has occurred.

Examples

To see the characteristics we have covered at work, let's explore two potential CMPEs. In these examples, I will invite you to try your hand at writing down and evaluating the parallels. It is all right if you don't do this, but please still read the examples.

Hard Ball

[Event 1] The new year had just arrived and Jim was attending a weekly class at church. That night, they were studying Jesus' parables and how they portrayed people as not being doomed to continue in the same old ruts, but free to let go of the past and head off in a new direction. At the end of the meeting, Jim and the others were led through an inner exercise in which they asked God two questions: "What old patterns would you like me to let go of?" and "How can you help me let these go?"

When Jim closed his eyes and asked the first question, he immediately got a picture of himself as a "hard-hearted person, a steel ball." The last few years of his life had been difficult. In response to all the conflict and misunderstanding, he had hardened and withdrawn. He silently asked for help in letting this go. As he drove home, he couldn't stop thinking about this. The phrase "hard-hearted steel ball" wouldn't leave his mind.

[Event 2] When he got home, his wife Beverly had just gotten off the phone with a friend. This friend was grappling with a chronic health challenge that, over the previous four years, had caused her life to virtually disintegrate. Beverly felt her friend needed to take a more spiritual approach to this. She suggested a healing process she had read about. This process saw illness as a manifestation of resentments over the past. It thus viewed healing as letting go of the past through forgiveness. Specifically, the process involved quieting your mind and asking for a picture that symbolizes your illness. Beverly said that for example, you might get a picture of a "hard, red ball in your knee." Then, once you get this picture, you ask for help from God to let it go. Upon hearing this, Jim was astonished. It was if he and his wife had attended the same class in different locations.

Now, if you will, take out a sheet of paper and try to list the parallels between events 1 and 2, making sure any item you list is an accurate description of both event 1 and event 2.

Once you have done that, evaluate the strength of your list by asking the following five questions. For this story to qualify as a genuine CMPE, you need to answer yes to *all* five questions. Please write your answers down as "yes," "no," or "maybe," and feel free to elaborate.

1. Are there one or more parallels that seem specific and unlikely?
2. Are there additional, more general parallels?
3. Is there a good number of total parallels—at least three and ideally around eight?
4. Does the list of parallels come together into a general situation or story?
5. Does the list as a whole capture something central about each event?

Now let's go on to my second example:

Change in Direction

An author tells this story:

"During a trip through the Southwest in 1982, I spent an afternoon with a Native American medicine man, a figure respected and feared by fellow villagers for his medicinal and magical knowledge. After talking for several hours about his practices and beliefs, he suggested we carry our conversation outside and take a walk along the edge of the village looking out over the desert.

[Event 1] "As we made our way along the sandy pathway, he asked about my life and interests back home in the Midwest. I started telling him about a project I was scheduled to become involved in....I related my suspicions that this effort appeared to be taking a much different direction than I had originally intended....

[Event 2] "Exactly at the moment I related my suspicions that this effort appeared to be taking a much different direction than I had originally intended, a bird conspicuously darted in front of us, letting out a sharp cry, only to change direction abruptly and make a sharp turn." [10]

At this point in the story, the medicine man remarked that, as the author thought, things were going to turn out quite differently than he originally planned. He explained that the "winged apparition" appearing at that precise moment was a message for the author. It was there to confirm his suspicions about the project. He concluded with the somber observation, "We have lost the capacity to interpret the signs from nature."

The medicine man felt this was a sign, but do you think this was a sign in the way that I am using the word—a CMPE? Try, then, to list the parallels between events 1 and 2, making sure any item you list is an accurate description of both event 1 and event 2.

Again, please write down the parallels between the two events and then write down your answers to the same five questions as before. Remember, for this to be a real sign, you need to answer all five questions in the affirmative.

1. Are there one or more parallels that seem specific and unlikely?
2. Are there additional, more general parallels?
3. Is there a good number of total parallels—at least three and ideally around eight?
4. Does the list of parallels come together into a general situation or story?
5. Does the list as a whole capture something central about each event?

Example #1: Hard Ball

Now I'll give you my answers. With the first example, "Hard Ball," I found nine parallels:

- Someone is asked by a teacher or advisor to do an inner process.
- This process involves closing one's eyes and asking within about a problem (either asking what problem should be addressed or asking for a picture of a particular problem).
- In this process, a picture of the problem comes to mind (in one case, it just happened to; in the other, it was supposed to).
- The picture is of a "hard ball" (in one case, that was the picture that came; in the other, that was an example of what might come).
- After that, the person asks for help from God in letting this problem go.
- The problem is understood to be, at root, some kind of holding onto the past (holding onto past "conflict and misunderstanding" or onto resentment over the past).

- The letting go is understood to be a letting go of the past.

- This person's problem is associated with a difficult recent past; he or she has experienced major life difficulties in the previous few years, and these are either the cause of the problem or the result of it.

- This person, therefore, has a great need to leave the past behind.

Did you find this many parallels? Parallels are not always easy to spot, but one problem is that you may not have looked long enough. One of the keys to finding the maximum number of parallels is to look until you feel sure you have exhausted them all—and then look some more.

Now for the evaluation:

1. *Are there one or more parallels that seem specific and unlikely?*

Yes, especially the one about seeing a picture of a hard ball as symbolizing the person's problem.

2. *Are there additional, more general parallels?*

Yes, the rest of the parallels are more general. They supply an overall shared context, such that the "hard ball" ends up being only the most prominent feature of an entire shared landscape.

3. *Is there a good number of total parallels—at least three and ideally around eight?*

Yes, there are nine, which is right around my average.

4. *Does the list of parallels come together into a general situation or story?*

Yes. The situation is this: A person is doing an inner exercise, which consists of asking within about a problem, getting a picture of the problem—as a hard ball—and asking God's help to let the problem go, which really means letting the *past* go, since the problem is some form of holding on to the past.

5. *Does the list as a whole capture something central about each event?*

Yes, the scenario I just sketched is at the heart of both Jim's class and

Beverly's conversation. The two events, in other words, have joined not at their periphery but at their core.

This is how you want a list of parallels to look. This is clearly a real CMPE. When you look at the entire list, and at the affirmative answers to the five questions, the idea that this convergence of events was mere chance seems severely strained. It would be one thing if there were only one parallel. Then we could say, OK, that was weird but it was probably just a fluke. But this goes way beyond one parallel. When two events resemble each other in all these ways, it is truly difficult to imagine their coming together is pure chance. You find yourself assuming that something *brought* them together. That is the effect a good list of parallels will have on you.

Example #2: Change in Direction

In this story I found only one parallel:

● Something changes direction.

If you got more than one parallel, check to make sure each parallel you got really did fit both events. To do so, you can draw up a table like the one below, in which you list the parallel in the left column and then list how that parallel shows up in event 1 (middle column) and how it shows up in event 2 (right column).

Parallel	Event 1	Event 2
Something changes direction.	The author suspected the project he would be involved in was taking a different direction than expected.	A bird darted in front of them but then abruptly changed direction.

Now for the evaluation:

1. *Are there one or more parallels that seem specific and unlikely?*
   No, the one parallel is very general and not unlikely at all. Things change direction all the time.

2. *Are there additional, more general parallels?*
    No.

3. *Are there a good number of total parallels—at least three and ideally around eight?*
    No.

4. *Does the list of parallels come together into a general situation or story?*
    No, one parallel is not enough to describe a situation or tell a story.

5. *Does the list as a whole capture something central about each event?*
    Perhaps. Certainly the notion of change of direction was central to the conversation (event 1). But was it central to the bird's flight (event 2)? We don't know, since we weren't there.

As you can see, this potential CMPE fails miserably. It does fit the more popular model of a sign, but it does not fit the model I am presenting in this book, not by a long way.

The wide gulf between these two examples reflects the typical distance between a genuine sign and a failed sign. I actually find very few borderline cases. Most cases are clearly out or clearly in. And when a case is clearly in, when it has passed all the tests, it leaves you with little doubt that you have witnessed something truly out of the ordinary.

Chapter 5
The Subject Situation

The Treasure House

Nicola and I had been receiving signs that said we needed to buy a home in Sedona for over a year, but nothing we looked at was right for us. Meanwhile, prices were soaring, and we were in danger of getting priced out of the market. Nicola was five months pregnant with our first child and the nesting instinct was strong. She wanted to be settled in our new home by the time the baby was born, but time was fast running out. One day, Nicola went with our realtor Jeff to look at homes within our price range and came back very distressed. She concluded that all we could afford at this point was a "pile of [blank]." That evening we had a long conversation about it and decided I needed to go back to our signs about the house and draw up a composite picture of what they had said. Maybe they could point us in the right direction.

I did this the next morning and became immediately convinced that Nicola needed to go back out and look at a house she had declined to view the day before because it was more than we could afford. From what Jeff told us, it fit almost all of the characteristics the signs had laid out—eight out of ten. We both ended up seeing it that day and it felt perfect. Against all the odds, here was the house we had been looking for. Jeff told us, however, that if we wanted it, we needed to put in an offer literally the next day. It had been priced to move and another offer was already on its way.

Though more than we could afford, the house was put within our reach by the fact that friends of ours had offered to own part of it as an investment. But the question still remained: Should we go ahead and buy it?

We went home after seeing it and prayed for guidance. Nicola's guidance made an interesting point. It emphasized that this place was like her "house dreams." These were a series of dreams that had come to her over a two-year period in which she found herself moving into a house with amazing size and potential. We had always wondered if these dreams were prophetic (since she had had prophetic dreams in the past), but over time they had slipped from our minds. So now, in the wake of Nicola's guidance, we pulled up the document I had written about them a year earlier. In it, I had recorded the dreams, catalogued their features, and tried to pull out the essence of the house they were describing. We had called this document "Treasure House Dreams" because the dreams reminded us of the image of the treasure house in *A Course in Miracles*.

Looking at the document, we realized the house we had seen that day was actually quite similar to her dreams. Just as in the dreams, the house was huge, with high ceilings, double doors, and lots of windows. And it had a labyrinthine feel to it, such that the more you explored it, the more you kept unexpectedly stumbling upon more rooms. Because the house fit these dreams and also fit our signs, because her guidance had given us the green light, and because the place just felt so right, we decided to go for it. We worked up an offer with our realtor that very night.

But we had really wanted a sign. I had been telling Nicola for a year that when we found the right place, we would probably have a sign about it that same day. But so far nothing had happened.

Then, after our realtor had gone home that evening, Nicola downloaded her e-mail…and announced that we had our sign. She had received the crucial e-mail from—of all people—*me*! Earlier that day, I had sent out to an e-mail list notes from a weekly class I was teaching. That week, however, there had been no class. So I had quickly looked through my folder of old class notes. A document titled "Treasury" jumped out at me, so I sent it out, and then forgot about it.

But now Nicola opened this document and looked at it more carefully. As it turns out, it was a study I had done a couple years earlier of the treasure house concept in *A Course in Miracles*! When we set it side by side with the document we had just pulled up about her dreams, we noticed a number of striking similarities. Both documents, of course, were about a "treasure house." In both, I had collected various images of this treasure house (in the Course or in Nicola's dreams), catalogued the house's features, and tried to draw together the essence of what the house is. (Yes, I realize I am a bit odd.)

And the houses themselves shared similarities (even though the treasure house in the Course is a place in the mind, not a physical house). These similarities were mainly between Nicola's key treasure house dream and the concluding visualization in my treasure house class notes. In both, we are going inside the treasure house for the first time. There are beings (either servants or angels) standing at the large front doors, welcoming people in. The house is described as "massive" and we are amazed at all the "opulence" or "splendor" we see. Yet as amazing as this house is, we find that it is *our* home. It has been given to us by an ancestor (either as an inheritance, in the dream, or as a gift from our Father, in the Course).

We were floored. Purely by "chance" we had before us two remarkably similar documents—one I had offhandedly sent out earlier in the day, and another that had been pointed out to us when we sought guidance that evening. It was an incredible sign, one that left us with no doubt this was the right house for us. We have been living here for three years now, and we love it. Every now and then we still look around and say, "What are we doing here? How did this happen?" And yes, we did get to move in before the baby was born!

CMPEs (*Conjunctions of Meaningfully Parallel Events*) are not just spectacular convergences of parallel events. They are aimed at a situation in our lives, usually some situation we are wrestling with at the time. I call this situation the *subject situation*. It is what the sign is addressing, what the sign is about.

How do you identify the subject situation? With most CMPEs it is intuitively obvious. You know immediately what the CMPE is about. However, as I mentioned earlier, there are rules for identifying it.

The essence of those rules is that there is a meeting place between where the sign itself is pointing and what is current and important in your life. The sign will point in a certain direction and you need to then see where that direction meets an actual situation in your life. I know this sounds vague right now, but I hope by the end of the chapter it will not.

In what follows, I will first describe a four-point process for identifying the subject situation and then walk you through an example of using the process.

1. Look for a situation in your life that fits the general pattern laid down by the parallels.

In the last chapter, I said that the parallels as a whole should describe a situation. This situation, however, will not be particularly specific. Rather, it will be more like a general pattern.

To find the specific subject situation, you need to find a situation in your life that fits this general pattern. By "in your life" I mean either a situation that is your own personal matter or a larger situation in which you are a participant.

This first point is the main guideline. The remaining three points merely help you narrow this one down.

2. It will be a situation that is most likely current, uncertain, unresolved, or at least needing confirmation—i.e., a situation in which you need counsel.

In addition to being in your life, the subject situation will probably be current, something you are dealing with right now. Being current, it will also probably be uncertain or unresolved, though sometimes it will be very recently resolved, but still in need of confirmation. All of this adds up to a simple idea: It is a situation in which you could use counsel.

This criterion is important. Sometimes there will be two situations in your life that fit the general pattern laid down by the parallels. How do you decide which is the actual subject situation? Almost certainly, one of the situations will be uncertain, unresolved, or current, while the other one will be over and done with. The first is the subject situation.

3. It will usually be contained in one (or both) events. Look there first.

The first place to look for a situation that fits the above guidelines is in the events of the sign itself. The subject situation is nearly always prominent in one or both events, often in the first event. Only in the rare case that you can't find the subject situation in the sign's events should you start casting your eye over your life as a whole.

4. It may be in the event that has the characteristics of an important event for you.

A large percentage of signs will contain at least one event that clearly has importance for you. When I say "importance for you," I specifically have in mind a list of characteristics that regularly show up in CMPE events:

- There is a **question** of yours that is central to one of the events, a question the sign could be seen as answering.
- There is a strongly felt **need, issue,** or **problem** of yours within one of the events.
- There is a **new idea, realization,** or **decision** of yours in one of the events. Signs will often come along and comment on new ideas or decisions, usually to confirm them (though occasionally to shoot them down).
- One of the events is **emotionally significant** for you—involving a major happening, an important piece of news, or a significant beginning, ending, or turning point.

When you see one of these characteristics in an event, you can be virtually certain that event contains the subject situation. Indeed, that characteristic is probably the specific focus of the CMPE. In other words, the CMPE is probably designed to *answer* that question or need, *confirm* that idea or decision, or *comment on* that emotionally significant occurrence. The CMPE will still be about the larger situation of which that characteristic is a part, but it will be *mainly* about the characteristic itself—about that question, need, idea, decision, or emotionally significant occurrence.

This fourth point is not only helpful for identifying the subject situation, it also tells us something about the nature of signs. Quite simply, signs gravitate to situations that are important to us. It is really quite astonishing just how many CMPEs contain the above characteristics. In fact, out of eight signs I have related so far, seven of them (the exception being the *Dora the Explorer* sign in Chapter 3) have an event with one or more of these characteristics. The remarkable prevalence of these characteristics implies that CMPEs don't address just any situation in our lives. Instead, they tend to focus on those situations that are important to us.

Example: "The Bucket Brigade"

To see this four-step process at work, let's go back to the story I told at the beginning of Chapter 1, "The Bucket Brigade." To refresh your memory of the events, the Circle of Atonement, a nonprofit spiritual teaching center, was going through a financial crisis. We asked within for guidance and then met to discuss it. Nicola received an inner picture in which people joined in a team effort to form a "chain gang" and were passing items quickly along the chain. This was happening in our mailroom, where we ship out our books and tapes. This "chain gang" was a symbol for us producing and distributing a particular book. Nicola was told that to get this book out properly, we needed to reexamine both the *who*—people's roles—and the *what*—the organization's activities. Setting aside normal roles and activities would allow us to weld ourselves into a chain that efficiently served a single goal, and this is what would solve our crisis. During our discussion of this guidance, I pointed out that her "chain gang" was usually called a "bucket brigade."

Shortly after my remark, we heard what sounded like falling water in a nearby room—the mailroom. We rushed in to discover that water was pouring through the unfinished ceiling onto the shipping table. We quickly moved the table aside and grabbed several large plastic buckets stacked next to it and arranged them in a row to catch the falling water (the water was coming through the ceiling in a straight line). Staff and volunteers left their duties to help. Everyone in the place mobilized to help with the cleanup.

To find the subject situation, we need to first generate a list of parallels. Here is the list I came up with:

- There is a crisis at the Circle of Atonement.

- The Circle staff mobilizes to respond to this crisis.

- The "who" changes—people leave their normal roles; their roles become determined by the crisis.

- The "what" changes—the Circle sets aside what it normally does and focuses on a single thing.

- Everyone works together as a team that serves a single goal.

- The staff forms a bucket brigade. They form a line of water-filled buckets.

- This happens in the mailroom.

- As a result, the crisis is averted.

Like any good list of parallels, this list outlines a situation, a situation that is not confined to one particular situation but is really more of a general pattern. The essence of that general pattern is this:

> There is a crisis at the Circle, in response to which everyone sets aside normal business, mobilizes as a team, and forms a bucket brigade, thus averting the crisis.

Our job now is to find a specific situation in the life of the group to which this sign occurred that fits this general pattern (point #1 above). This situation should also be current, uncertain, unresolved, or at least needing confirmation (point #2).

The first place we look, of course, is in the events of the sign itself (point #3). The two events were:

1. Our discussion of the bucket brigade guidance
2. Our clean-up of the water leak

If we have to pick which of these two events was current, uncertain, unresolved, or at least needing confirmation, the choice is obvious: event 1. It represented an issue that was still open. The guidance had laid before us a daring plan for the future and we hadn't decided if we were going to enact that plan or not. Furthermore, the larger situation we were meeting about—our financial crisis—was still very much in force. In contrast, after a few minutes, the water cleanup was really over. The repairman who had turned the wrong knob simply turned it back. Why on earth would we need counsel about *that*?

This gets even clearer when we look at the fourth point: Was one of the events an important event for us? Did one of them have any of those characteristics I listed above? Again the answer is event 1. Indeed, event 1 actually had most of the characteristics I listed. We had a major *problem* on our hands (the financial crisis). We were discussing a *new idea* designed to solve the problem (Nicola's guidance). We had a *question*: Should we follow this guidance? And the entire thing was *emotionally significant*: We were faced not only with a crisis, but with a solution that looked hopeful yet that also challenged our entire organizational way of being.

Clearly, the subject situation is contained in event 1. It is Nicola's guidance about our financial crisis, and more specifically, it is the question of the validity of that guidance, a question that was uppermost in our minds.

But then you surely already assumed all that from the start. You almost certainly took one look at the bucket brigade story and thought, "It's confirming what that woman's guidance said." How many people would have assumed, "It's telling them how to clean up that water leak"? Somehow, we already get the logic behind the four-point process I laid out, and we apply that logic intuitively and instantly.

For this reason, I am not going to include an exercise at the end of this chapter (though the exercise at the end of the next chapter will include identifying the subject situation).

Conclusion

If we can identify the subject situation intuitively, why do we even need the four-point process I have outlined? There are two reasons. First, it makes the point that this phenomenon operates by rules. It is not an inkblot onto which we can just project our unconscious expectations. Second, there is a minority of signs in which finding the subject situation is more tricky. For those, these rules will come in handy.

All genuine signs have a subject situation. In fact, this is really the final criterion for calling something a genuine sign. If you don't have a subject situation, you don't have a sign. That being said, however, if you don't have a subject situation, you almost certainly have a weak set of parallels as well. In my experience, if the parallels are strong, the subject situation will be there.

The presence of the subject situation casts new light on the nature of the phenomenon we are discussing. Quite simply, it suggests a phenomenon that is responsive to our needs. CMPEs do not just come to any situations. They come to situations that are important to us (point #4 above) and in which we need counsel (point #2). They come where we have a need. This is not uniformly apparent. Sometimes I am mystified by how they repeatedly address a situation that seems peripheral while ignoring one in which I feel intense need. Yet by and large, you can see them gravitating to situations in which you need their guidance. Rightly or wrongly, they convey the distinct impression you are being seen and spoken to.

Chapter 6
Interpretation

The Truth of Symbolism

Nicola and I had been talking about how to present in this book the topic of symbolism (which will be covered in the current chapter). She had repeatedly shared her concerns about the potential for misunderstanding that would be opened up as soon as I mentioned the word "symbolism," and wondered if I could use a different word or even avoid the topic altogether. She settled on the idea that I needed a lengthy section in which I anticipated the misunderstandings that would arise and thoroughly clarified the issue. I initially didn't see the problem, yet the more we talked the more I realized she was right—the topic of symbolism in CMPEs is a veritable minefield of potential misunderstanding. These concerns provide the setting for the sign that occurred.

Event 1. While writing a draft of Chapter 1 of this book, I introduce a caution about symbolism.

Several months after Nicola and I began discussing the symbolism issue, I was working on an early draft of this book's first chapter. In that draft, I told the bucket brigade story and then mentioned that "the cleanup is not literal; it is a symbolic event." Then I wrote:

> A caution about symbolism: To understand how symbolism works in signs, you have to virtually throw out all your preconceptions about symbolism.

I was about to explain that the right way vs. the wrong way would be discussed at length in the chapter on interpretation. By this time I had come to agree with Nicola's points and therefore planned to devote several pages in that chapter to clarifying how symbolism in signs works differently than how we normally understand symbolism. However, before I wrote any more, I decided to take a brief break.

Event 2. I read a section titled "The Truth of Metaphor" in *The Heart of Christianity.*

On my break, I picked up a book I was reading by Marcus Borg, titled *The Heart of Christianity*. I opened to my bookmark and read the beginning of a section titled "The Truth of Metaphor." Borg's point in this section was that we should approach the stories of the Bible as metaphor. Whether those stories really happened or not, their primary value for us lies in the metaphorical truths they convey about the human condition and the divine-human relationship. Those are the truths that can provide wisdom for our lives.

Yet, Borg says, this perspective runs smack up against our culture's prevailing love affair with factual truth, which asks only one question: Did those stories really happen? From this standpoint, approaching the Bible as metaphor means demoting it to the status of less-than-literal. Borg, however, spends eight pages arguing that metaphorical really means "more-than-literal." This is because the meaning that biblical stories carry for our lives is, in the end, more important than their factual truth. This implies that even when a story *is* factual, "its more-than-literal meaning matters most."[11] Unfortunately, though, in our obsession with factuality, the Bible's "rich, more-than-literal meanings are most often lost."[12] This is why Borg spends so much time on this, because what is at stake is nothing less than our ability to lay hold of the gifts contained in the stories of the Bible.

I immediately recognized that this was a sign. Borg, after all, was talking about symbolism—metaphor is symbolic language—just as I was. Even more striking, the central tension in his discussion felt exactly the same as in mine. This feeling was confirmed when I wrote out the parallels, drawing on what Borg wrote and what Nicola and I had planned for me to write.

Parallels

- An author is writing a book.
- He is writing about how to approach stories that have traditionally been seen (Bible stories) or can be seen (CMPEs) as communications from a higher source. [13]
- He is writing about how to get from these stories the meaning they contain for our lives.
- In particular, he is writing a section about how to unlock their symbolism.
- His approach to symbolism, however, is poles apart from the approach that is deeply ingrained in the culture.
- He therefore spends many pages arguing for his approach and contrasting it with the prevailing approach, struggling to overcome that deeply ingrained mindset.
- The issue is crucial, for his approach, he claims, can unlock the meaning these stories have for our lives, while the prevailing approach threatens to obscure that meaning.

The odds against planning to write a discussion that fit all these points, and seconds later *reading* such a discussion (which I had no idea was coming in the book), seemed astronomical. The discussions were just too similar.

As you might imagine, I took this as confirmation of the plan to thoroughly clarify the subject of symbolism in this chapter. It wasn't only Nicola and I who felt there was a potential danger here that needed to be addressed at length. The signs clearly agreed.

We have now come to the final point in our four-point model: interpretation. If a CMPE (*Conjunction of Meaningfully Parallel Events*) has passed all the tests so far—if it has a solid pair of events, a strong set of parallels, and a subject situation—then it *will* have an interpretation. It will have a message.

This final point is what all the previous points have been leading up to, for, of course, what we want are those messages. We want guidance for our lives. And CMPEs appear to be designed to provide that guidance. I realize this is a strong claim, but it grows directly out of the basic structure of signs. That basic structure first *highlights* a situation and then *portrays* it in a certain way. CMPEs, in other words, appear to be designed to say something about situations in our lives.

Here in this final point is where the signs really shine. Yes, the parallels are impressive, yet what I find equally impressive, and far more important, is the quality of the counsel communicated by the signs. As we will see in Part II, the guidance they offer appears to be of a very high quality.

But we are getting ahead of ourselves. In this chapter, we will focus simply on how we derive the interpretation. As with the previous points, the process is rule-based. There is a definite message contained in the CMPE itself. In the process of interpreting, our entire focus is on trying to identify that message. We want to consciously set aside our own desires and assumptions and let the CMPE speak for itself. It may say something to our liking and it may not. It may confirm what we wanted to hear and it may come up with a new idea that never occurred to us. Either way, we should treat it as we would a person who was trying to get a point across to us. We would want to get that person's point, not just hear what we wanted to hear.

Therefore, in working with a sign, try to let the interpretation arise spontaneously from the workings of the rules. There is a beauty to a thought process that simply allows the truth to arise, as a pure product of the evidence, untainted by any personal wishes. Let your interpretation contain that beauty, and the treasures of the signs will be yours.

1. How do the parallels and symbolism frame the subject situation?

This is the essence of interpreting a CMPE. Patterns within the CMPE itself—parallels (which we have discussed) and symbolism (which we will soon discuss)—frame the subject situation in a certain way. Our task is simply to identify that way. The following three points will help us do that.

2. How do the parallels and symbolism address our specific concern within the subject situation?

While interpreting, we often need to pay special attention to our specific concern within the subject situation. In the previous chapter, I talked about what I called "the characteristics of an important event." I said that one of the events in the sign might contain a vital *question*, a strongly felt *need*, *issue*, or *problem*, a new *idea*, *realization*, or *decision*, or a significant *beginning*, *ending*, or *turning point*. If so, that characteristic represents what I am here calling our *specific concern*. This specific concern is what the sign will be addressing in particular. The sign will still address the subject situation in general, but it will also address this characteristic in particular. It will, for instance, be *answering* the question or problem, or *confirming* the new idea or decision.

What I have yet to explain, of course, is how the parallels and symbols have the ability to frame the subject situation and address our specific concern. I turn to that now.

3. See the parallels as confirming aspects of the subject situation.

We have already seen that the parallels play a crucial role in identifying that something is a genuine CMPE, and a similarly crucial role in identifying the subject situation. Their final role lies in communicating the sign's message.

How do they do that? The simple answer is that parallels are an implied *confirmation*. They confirm the elements of the subject situation they highlight. They carry an implicit message: "There is something right or true about this element."

The kind of confirmation varies a bit according to what actually needs to be confirmed. With some parallels, what needs confirmation is what the parallel implies we should do, in which case that is what is confirmed. For instance, one of the parallels in the bucket brigade sign (Chapter 1) was "The staff forms a bucket brigade." When you read that, I think you intuitively recognize that it's confirming that, yes, we *should* do that.

In other cases, what needs to be confirmed is whether or not what the parallel says is true. This was the case with the parallel "The father's work is significantly cutting into his family time" in "Family Comes First" (Chapter

4). That parallel was simply confirming that, yes, my work time really was compromising my family time.

Then there are some parallels for which confirmation is irrelevant because the parallels are purely incidental. In "Family Comes First," this was true of the parallel, "At the holiday celebration...someone sets off firecrackers." All that parallel really did was strengthen the overall list of parallels, which is true of many parallels.

I think on some level we immediately understand all of this when we look at a list of parallels. It just feels like the CMPE is backing up or validating those items on the list, especially the more substantial ones. And that, in my experience, is exactly how CMPEs behave.

4. See the symbolism as commenting on aspects of the subject situation.

Thus far I have said very little about symbolism in CMPEs, but I have now reached the point at which I need to carry out the advice of that sign I shared at the beginning of the chapter. Therefore, I will first explain how symbolism works in CMPEs and then clarify how that differs from the more conventional understanding.

To begin with, it is probably best to think not in terms of individual symbols (though I will speak in these terms later in the book) but in terms of what I call the *symbolic situation*. The symbolic situation is the situation in the events of the sign that *parallels* the subject situation but is *not* the subject situation.

I realize that's a mouthful, but it's really a very simple concept. In most signs, one of the events will contain the subject situation (what the sign is about). The other event will contain a situation that closely mirrors the subject situation, but is still an entirely different situation. We have already seen a number of examples of this.

In "The Bucket Brigade" (Chapter 1), the subject situation was Nicola's guidance recommending that we form a bucket brigade to solve our financial crisis. This was contained in event 1. Event 2—dealing with the water leak—contained a situation that was eerily parallel yet still entirely different. Dealing with the water leak was clearly the *symbolic situation*.

In "Krusty the Father" (Chapter 3), the subject situation was again in event 1: me taking my son to play Frisbee as a way to get back in touch with my priorities as a father. Then event 2—the *Simpsons* episode—again contained an uncannily parallel yet entirely different situation: Krusty the Clown taking his newfound daughter to the beach. That was the symbolic situation.

I hope you can see this is a very simple concept. The symbolic situation *parallels but is not* the subject situation. Not every sign has a symbolic situation, since sometimes the subject situation is in *both* events. But most do, and when they do, more often than not it is in the second event.

The symbolic situation, when present, is the other major communicator of the sign's message. Quite simply, the symbolic situation *comments on* the subject situation. Just as the parallels are authoritative confirmation of aspects of the subject situation, so the symbolic situation is *authoritative commentary* on the subject situation.

It is not hard to see how the symbolic situation does this. All the CMPE is doing is setting next to your situation some other situation that, in the eyes of the CMPE, contains the *truth* about yours. We do the same thing ourselves all the time. Imagine a teenage girl talking to her mother. "Mom," she says, "I think I want to break up with my boyfriend. He seems kind of boring, and there's this really hot guy in my chemistry class that I'm hoping will notice me." In response, her mother might tell a kind of parable: "You know, when I was your age, I had a boyfriend who wasn't as exciting as I would have liked. So I almost broke it off. But I finally realized his many fine qualities and decided to stick with him. And we have been happily married these last twenty years."

The signs are doing the exact same thing. Here we are, wondering if we should form a bucket brigade to solve our financial crisis, and the sign sets next to us a situation in which we *have* to form a bucket brigade. Here I am, feeling like I've been a neglectful father who needs to spend more time with his kids, and the sign sets next to me a situation in which a really neglectful father decides to be a better one.

That, very simply, is how symbolism works in signs. As we wrestle with some situation in our lives, the sign sets right next to it a parable, a story that is clearly like our situation yet that also is meant to convey the truth about our situation.

These symbolic situations have a great deal more flexibility in what they can say than the parallels do. While the parallels merely confirm, the symbolic situation has a greater range of commentary it can offer. Often it does simply confirm or reinforce something uncertain, but it can also answer questions, correct mistaken ideas, make predictions, and even offer novel solutions or plans of action. Here in the symbolism, then, is where signs possess their greatest freedom to comment on our lives.

Symbolism in CMPEs vs. symbolism as normally understood

How does what I just described differ from the conventional approach to symbolism? To answer that, we first need to understand the conventional approach. In our usual thinking, a symbol is a simple object that possesses a number of pre-set meanings, so that whenever that object shows up, it carries one of those meanings. For example, according to an online symbol dictionary, "grape" can mean the following things:

- Abundance, richness, fullness
- Prosperity
- Fertility or ova
- Being a bad loser, a sour grape

Thus, whenever a grape shows up as a symbol, it will represent abundance, prosperity, fertility, or sour grapes.

From this perspective, then, symbols function just like words, in that a given word, of course, also has a pre-set list of meanings, so that whenever that word is used, it will express one of those meanings. If you look up the *word* "grape," for instance, you find that it can refer to the fruit, to the vine, to the color, or to "grapeshot" (the cannon version of buckshot). Symbols, then, in our typical understanding, function just like words. They are a kind of picture language, which of course is why there are symbol dictionaries.

My problem with this usual view of symbols is two-fold. First, how do you know that object means anything? If I open my refrigerator and a grape drops out, how do I know that grape has any symbolic meaning whatsoever? If I assume it means that today I will have prosperity (one of the symbolic meanings of "grape"), how do I know I am not falling prey to sheer superstition?

Second, even if I assume the symbol does mean something, how do I know which, *if any*, of its meanings apply in this particular case? How do I know, for example, that the grape falling out of the fridge is not telling me I'm a bad loser ("sour grapes")? How do I know the appropriate meaning is even on the list? Maybe "grape" can have additional meanings not listed. Or maybe the entire list is wrong. Who makes up these lists anyway?

My problem, in short, is that I can see no good reason to decide *what* these symbols mean or *that* they mean anything. It all seems so hopelessly subjective. If we were to import this approach into CMPEs, we would have complete chaos.

For example, let's look at the King Kong sign (Chapter 2). In that sign are a few images that strike one as likely symbols in the conventional sense: gorilla, party, movie. Yet each of these, of course, has multiple possible meanings. For instance, according to entries for "gorilla" and "ape" in different symbol dictionaries, that symbol could stand for wisdom, or mischief and curiosity, or communication and expression, or inner strength and nobility, or generosity, or fear of expressing one's individuality, or clowning around, or copying someone ("aping"), or going crazy (going ape), or primal power, or primitive development, or immature intelligence.

If we then look at the entire cluster of *gorilla*, *party*, and *movie*, the sign could possibly mean that this is a time of joy, festivity, and cheer (party), and yet you are complacent, holding others responsible for your entertainment (movie). Therefore, start clowning around. Display more primal energy (gorilla). Or maybe I didn't read the symbols correctly. Here is another possible interpretation: You are being a party to something you shouldn't be (party). Instead, you should step back and observe the roles you play in life (movie) and cultivate more wisdom and inner strength (gorilla). One could go on developing who-knows-how-many additional interpretations. I personally have no idea how you actually settle on one in particular.

The problem, however, is far more basic: We don't even know if gorilla, party, and movie had *any* symbolic meaning in the King Kong sign. And in fact, by the rules of CMPEs, they didn't. They didn't mean a thing.

In CMPEs, symbols are not simple objects. Rather, they are *complex situations*. Look, for instance, at the "Truth of Symbolism" sign above. There, the symbol is not something simple like "gorilla" or "grape." Rather, it is an entire multifaceted situation: Marcus Borg is urging his readers to approach biblical stories metaphorically, in order to get from them the meaning they carry for our lives, and is contrasting this with the more conventional approach to those stories, which he believes obscures their real import for our lives. That *whole* situation is the symbol.

Furthermore, this symbol doesn't carry a list of pre-set meanings. Indeed, so far as the signs are concerned, it wasn't a symbol at all until it was *set alongside the subject situation*—my parallel situation of writing about symbolism in signs. Its *existence* as a symbol and its *meaning* as a symbol arise solely from its proximity to the subject situation.

This approach to symbolism, I believe, solves the two problems I mentioned above. First, in contrast to symbolism as normally understood, we can be far more confident that this symbol really does mean something. Its appearance next to an uncannily parallel situation of mine sure seems like more than chance. It seems intentional. It seems *meaningful*.

Second, in contrast to my gorilla example, I think we can also be confident about *what* this symbol means. Remember, its meaning is determined by its relationship with the subject situation, so let's look there first. In the subject situation, I had processed at length the question of how to handle the topic of symbolism. Do I leave it out? If I include it, how do I avoid misunderstanding? I had finally come to a decision: explain it at length while contrasting it with the usual approach to symbolism. This decision represents what I earlier called my *specific concern*. I had made a decision, but was it correct or not?

Then, right as I expressed that decision in writing, I encountered another situation that was strikingly parallel to mine—yet not entirely parallel. On my side, I was just beginning to carry out a relatively recent decision in my initial draft of the beginning of a book. In contrast, on the side of the symbol, a writer I greatly respect was making a very cogent argument in a book that was already written and already published. The symbol, then, had the aura of finality and rightness, whereas the actual subject situation was fresh and tentative. If we take the symbolic situation as authoritative commentary on my decision, then it is clearly saying that *my* decision should be regarded as final and right.

This relationship between the subject situation and the symbolic situation is where the meaning of the symbol comes from. In this case, we had an unconfirmed decision set next to a symbol that looked both final and right. In other cases, there is a problem set next to what looks like a solution. In still other cases, there is a new idea set next to what appears to be a refutation of that idea. And even when there is no decision, problem, or new idea present—no specific concern—the symbolic situation is still telling a story that frames the subject situation in a particular way.

In all of these cases, the idea is the same: Treat the symbolic situation as implied commentary on the subject situation. Treat it as a parable about the subject situation. Give it the authority to frame the subject situation however it wants. But never—and I mean *never*—try to determine its meaning by cracking open a symbol dictionary.

Summary

Interpretation in principle is a fairly simple affair. On the one side, you have a situation in your life—the subject situation. This is what the sign is addressing, especially any specific concern you have regarding this situation, any question, problem, realization, decision, or turning point that may have been present in the events of the sign.

Then, on the other side, you have the parallels and symbolism. They convey the sign's commentary on your situation. The parallels are there to confirm the aspects of the subject situation they highlight. The symbolic situation is there to act as a parable that comments on the subject situation, that frames it in a certain way. These two sources always work together, and between the two of them (although some signs only have the parallels), the CMPE presents an overall perspective on the situation in your life, a perspective designed to address your specific concern (if you had one).

With perhaps most signs, if you have done good work on the parallels and subject situation, the interpretation will virtually jump out at you. That is the case with almost all of the examples I've presented so far in this book. That being said, however, there are depths and intricacies to sign interpretation that make some signs hard to penetrate and can add extra richness to even the most obvious signs. These depths arise from patterns within the parallels and symbolism and how those patterns interact with each other and with the subject situation.

My advice for now, however, is to forget the depths and intricacies. Just go for the main thrust, that obvious interpretation that jumps out at you when you finish identifying the parallels and subject situation. Working with the depths in a reliable manner takes a combination of natural aptitude, training, and experience. Without that, I shudder to think of what esoteric nonsense one might pull out of a sign. So, expect that the depths are there, but aim instead for the sign's simple and unmistakable main point. Worry about the depths when you have more experience under your belt.

Exercise

For this our final exercise, I am going to give you the events of a sign, identify the parallels for you, and then leave you to both find the subject situation and try your hand at an interpretation. I think you'll find this is easier than you suspect. Even if you don't do the exercise, I urge you to read through the material, as it will help you understand how interpretation works.

Baby Sign Language

Event 1. Nicola tells me about the *Baby Signs* book.

Since our daughter Miranda was born Nicola and I had been toying with the idea of using baby sign language. We had heard about the discovery, which is relatively recent, that babies are able to communicate through sign language before they can actually talk. But we were hesitant. I guess we were uncertain it would really work, or at least work enough in our case to make it worthwhile. We even worried that a baby's reliance on sign language can delay her beginning to speak. Finally, when Miranda was nine months old, Nicola bought a book called *Baby Signs: How to Talk with Your Baby Before Your Baby Can Talk*. Once she began reading it, she couldn't wait to sit down with me and share what she had been learning. The stories in the book demonstrated what an endorsement on the back of the book says: "Babies are a lot smarter about language than we thought, and long before they can talk they can speak in symbols and gestures." Nicola told me a couple of these stories, which were simply amazing. Here is one that she shared:

> Nineteen-month-old Micah and his dad were window-shopping in the mall when something attracted Micah's attention. He suddenly became very excited and started doing his Baby Signs for bird and horse, one right after the other. "Oh, you see a birdie and a horsie?" his Dad responded. But Micah shook his head no and continued doing the two Baby Signs together. Then Micah's dad realized what Micah was "talking" about. "Bird-horses!" said his Dad with a grin. And indeed, that's exactly what Micah had spotted. Hanging from the ceiling in one of the stores was a large mobile made up of brightly colored, winged unicorns flying around and around. Far from being stymied by the fact that *unicorn* was not in his vocabulary, Micah had created his own, very sensible, compound Baby Signs word.[14]

This story, along with the other information from the book that Nicola shared, gave both of us a strong feeling that baby sign language really works. It felt like a significant moment. We came away expecting we would be able to have definite, intentional communication with our daughter well before she could talk. Our minds were made up. We decided to teach Miranda baby signs.

Event 2. I am sent an e-mail about monkey language.

About four hours later, I was sent an e-mail as part of a news service I subscribe to. It was titled, "Pyow pyow pyow . . . hack hack hack hack! Let's get out of here (in monkey talk)."[15] The article reports an important new discovery in the ability of animals to generate language. Here is how it begins:

> Monkeys are able to string together a simple "sentence," according to research that offers the first evidence that animals might be capable of a key feature of language.
>
> British scientists have discovered that the putty-nosed monkey in Nigeria pictured above sometimes communicates by combining sounds into a sequence that has a different meaning from any of its component calls, an ability that was thought to be uniquely human.

The article went on to discuss the two sounds put together by these monkeys:

> The putty-nosed monkeys, Cercopithecus nictitans, of the Gashaka Gumti National Park, have two main alarm call sounds. A sound known onomatopoeically as the "pyow" warns other animals against a lurking leopard, and a cough-like sound that scientists call a "hack" is used when an eagle is hovering near by.
>
> Kate Arnold and Klaus Zuberbühler, of the University of St Andrews, have now observed the monkeys using these sounds in a new way. A particular sequence of pyows and hacks appears to mean something entirely different.
>
> The monkeys live in groups consisting of a single adult male accompanied by several adult females and their young. When the male utters this "sentence," consisting of up to three pyows followed by up to four hacks, it seems to be a command telling others to move, generally to find safer, less exposed terrain.
>
> They use the signal not only when predators are around, but also during ordinary activities such as foraging. It seems to mean "let's get out of here."

As you can probably see, we have a solid pair of events here: two distinct events, causally independent (one didn't cause the other, neither seem caused by a third event), within hours of each other (four, to be exact), and strikingly similar.

The real strength of the CMPE comes out when we look at the parallels. Here is the list I compiled:

- I read about a new (or relatively new) discovery.
- It reveals that some creature thought to be too undeveloped for language has a greater capacity for language than previously thought.
- The creature's primitive language consists of something other than normal human language (in one case, it is sign language; in the other case, it is meaningful sounds).
- This creature has shown the ability to put symbols together on its own.
- The example given was one in which this creature on its own put two symbols together to produce a completely new meaning.
- One symbol stood for a large mammal (horse, leopard).
- The other symbol stood for a bird (bird, eagle).

Though not stunning, this is a strong list of parallels. It follows the classic pattern of specific, unlikely parallels (a creature creating a new "word" by putting together the symbols for a large mammal and a bird) set within an overall parallel context (a new discovery reveals that some creature is more capable of language than was thought; it can combine different symbols on its own). The parallels also come together to sketch a general situation— you can see this situation just by reading down the list. Finally, that situation goes to the heart of each of the events. Here, then, we have everything we want from a list of parallels.

Subject situation

Now let's find the subject situation, what the sign is about. Below I have listed the rules from the last chapter. Note that I've changed the wording to apply to me since I was the one the sign happened to.

1. Look for a situation in my life that fits the general pattern (or general situation) laid down by the parallels.
2. Look for a situation that was most likely current, uncertain, unresolved, or at least needing confirmation—i.e., a situation in which I needed counsel.
3. Look first in the events of the sign. The subject situation will usually be contained in one (or both) of them.
4. Look for an event that has the characteristics of an important event for me (a vital question, issue, need, problem, new idea, realization, decision, important piece of news, or significant happening, beginning, ending, or turning point). If such an event is there, the subject situation will be in it.

Now please take out a piece of paper and write down what you believe is the subject situation. Be sure to include any of the characteristics from the fourth step that apply.

Interpretation

Having identified the subject situation, let's see if you can write an interpretation. To walk you through the process, I am going to reorder and slightly expand the points we covered in this chapter.

1. See the parallels as confirming the aspects of the subject situation they highlight.

If the parallels are there to confirm aspects of the subject situation, what do you think *this* list of parallels confirms about *this* subject situation? Don't worry about using all the parallels, just those that seem to confirm something relevant about the subject situation. Write down your answer.

2. Identify the symbolic situation, if there is one.

Before we can work with the symbolism, we have to find out what it is. We have to identify the symbolic situation, if there is one. Like the subject situation, the symbolic situation fits the general pattern laid down by the parallels. Yet unlike the subject situation, it is either not a situation in my life or is not a current situation in which I need counsel.

Look for a situation in this sign that fits these parameters. Do you find one? If so, what is it? Again, write your answers down.

3. See the symbolic situation as providing authoritative commentary on the subject situation.

If the symbolic situation is a kind of parable that represents the truth of the subject situation, what is *this* symbolic situation saying about *this* subject situation? If it is simply confirming the subject situation, you can use the same answer you used for #1 above. If you believe it is saying something new, write that down.

4. What do the parallels and symbolic situation say about Robert's specific concern within the subject situation?

To answer this, you will need to have first identified my specific concern, which is represented by any of those "characteristics of an important event for me" that you identified in the fourth step of the subject situation process.

If you did identify a specific concern of mine in the subject situation, what do you think the parallels and symbolic situation are saying about that specific concern? Again, write down your answer.

5. How are the parallels and symbolism framing the subject situation and addressing my specific concern?

Answering this question equals writing an interpretation. So go ahead and do that. Take your answers to questions 1, 3, and 4 above, and weave them together into a single coherent interpretation.

Answer key

Here is what I came up with:

Subject situation

The subject situation is baby sign language, both the general validity of it and specifically my and Nicola's decision to teach it to our daughter.

Interpretation

1.   The parallels confirm the following about the subject situation: A relatively new discovery reveals that preverbal babies have a greater capacity for language than previously thought. They can not only use sign language, but can even put signs together to create new meanings.

2.   The symbolic situation is monkey language, the newly-discovered ability of certain monkeys to not only use sounds to communicate, but to combine different sounds to create new meanings.

3.   The commentary provided by the symbolic situation is basically confirmation of the subject situation, so it yields the same results as in question 1.

4.   My specific concern was my and Nicola's *decision* to teach our daughter baby sign language. The parallels and symbols are confirming the rightness of this decision.

5.   Overall interpretation: Baby signs really do work. They work because babies have a greater capacity for language than we commonly assume. They even have the capacity to form novel meanings by combining individual signs that they are taught. Therefore, we don't need to be uncertain about them. Nicola's and my decision to use baby signs with our daughter was correct.

I hope your answer was in the same general ballpark as mine. Even if it wasn't, I hope you can see that this process is rule-based. Two different interpreters using the same rules should come up with basically the same interpretation. To reinforce this point, I have included Greg Mackie's interpretation of this CMPE. Greg did the same exercise you did, but had to start from scratch. All he had was the account of the two events, which means he had to come up with his own list of parallels—probably the hardest part. Here is Greg's interpretation:

Your (Robert and Nicola's) decision to teach Miranda baby sign language is correct. Baby sign language really works, because the language ability of babies is more advanced than you had previously thought. They are capable of language even though they are incapable of human speech. Therefore, teaching Miranda baby sign language will enable you to have definite, intentional communication with her before she learns to talk.

To see how similar our two interpretations are, read through this comparison of key sentences in them:

Robert's interpretation	Greg's interpretation
Baby signs really do work.	Baby sign language really works.
They work because babies have a greater capacity for language than we commonly assume.	[It] works, because the language ability of babies is more advanced than you had previously thought.
Therefore, we don't need to be uncertain about them [baby signs].	Therefore, teaching Miranda baby sign language will enable you to have definite, intentional communication with her before she learns to talk.
Nicola's and my decision to use baby signs with our daughter was correct.	Your (Robert and Nicola's) decision to teach Miranda baby sign language is correct.

The similarity is quite striking, but by now this shouldn't surprise you. In fact, you probably came up with something similar yourself. You probably even intuited this message right from the start. The point of all this agreement is obvious: The message we are seeing here is not only in our minds. It is in the structure of the CMPE itself. We are hearing a message that the CMPE itself is conveying.

Chapter 7
The Interconnectedness of CMPEs

Two Fundraising Letters

It was October 31, 2003, and at the Circle of Atonement we were trying to craft a letter to send to major supporters. We were hoping they would donate the funds needed to publish *Path of Light*, the introductory book recommended in the bucket brigade sign (Chapter 1).

That day, one of our board members wanted to talk to me about this fundraising letter. He said that instead of calling on people to respond to our need, as we had been planning, we should call upon their "heart connection" with our vision. He reiterated this in an e-mail message afterwards:

> The point was that people don't give to causes or organizations because of need, they give because they have some emotional connection, some heart connection. This really seems clear when you consider all the real needs for funds that go unmet in the world. So I think the point is to try to invite people to become a part of the big vision that you have for [*Path of Light*] and its effect on *A Course in Miracles* in the world.

At the same time that I was at the Circle speaking with this board member, Nicola was at home being struck with a "sense that there was guidance wanting to come through." In response to this, she sat down and wrote the following:

> Our concerted message to the Course world isn't that we are poor and need financial aid. It is that we carry enormous rich- es for the Course world, and are devoted to the task of seeing

that the Course's message reaches the hearts for whom it was intended. People will give to us, not in direct proportion to the specific gifts we are giving, but because they recognize the priceless value of our role....They give out of a sense of a deep connection with what we are truly about.

She then wrote that this guidance was meant to be applied to that same fundraising letter.

It was clearly a sign. The two pieces of advice (from the board member and from Nicola's guidance) said virtually the same thing. The message was a novel one for us (though we have since discovered that it's common knowledge among fundraisers), and resulted in a new direction for the fundraising letter. Here is how I interpreted that message:

People will give to us, not because of a specific need or specific service, but because they see that we are fulfilling our purpose of bringing the Course to the world, a purpose that they too believe in. Our letter to major donors should reflect this fact.

Three years later, in 2006, we were again trying to write a fundraising letter, this time a year-end plea to our entire list. We hoped to attract people to give each month for a year, and to this end we had devised a rather complicated series of "freebies." People giving at various levels per month would receive a free book, CD, e-book, or some combination of these.

Nicola, however, couldn't shake a bad feeling about this plan, which would not let her rest until she wrote an e-mail to the board. In it, she said, "I couldn't help get a gut feeling that this is not the way to go." She said that we should be "attracting people because of our vision and not the freebies. Here we have a complex hierarchy of freebies. It just seems—well, not quite right." She went on to address the details of the plan, including the free book and CD that had been proposed, and eliciting monthly giving.

Fifteen minutes after getting all this off her chest, Nicola sat down to read *Organizing for Dummies* by Eileen Roth and Elizabeth Miles, as part of an effort to get our house organized. The authors were complaining about how people tend to measure themselves "not on the basis of inner riches or personal fulfillment but by the number of things in their houses and yards," and how advertisers take advantage of this. Then, to Nicola's shock, the book launched into a warning about freebies:

Freebies

Even more appealing than a sale to our bargain-hunting soul is that other four-letter word: free....But free offers usually have a price. Either the item comes attached to something else that you have to buy and might not want, or you have to buy more later...

Then there are the notorious offers where you get a free book or CD if you agree to buy ten more during the year. Would you buy ten books otherwise? Do they have the books you want?

The two messages—from Nicola and from these two authors—were just too similar. It had to be a CMPE. In both cases, someone is writing a piece that is against the use of "freebies" to elicit buying or giving. Both pieces criticize the use of books and CDs as freebies, especially as a way to compel multiple-installment giving or buying over a year. Finally, both say that it should be about more intangible things, like "inner riches" or "our vision." Here is the interpretation I wrote:

Nicola is right about the fundraising letter. It needs to not be so focused on freebies. Instead, it needs to elicit giving because people are attracted to our vision.

Of course, this new sign immediately reminded Nicola and me of the one from three years before. The two signs were incredibly similar. Both were about how the Circle should compose a fundraising letter. Both affirmed that the letter should elicit giving based on a connection with our vision, not based on some specific thing people get. And in both, this message comes in part from Nicola as a result of some inner urge or compulsion. The two signs were so much alike that each one looked more like the other than it looked like any other sign we had ever received.

That's when we realized it: Today was October 31. This second sign had happened on the exact same day that, three years earlier, the first sign had!

We have completed our tour of the four-point model. We can now take a quick backward glance at it and then move on. In the end, the model is fairly simple:

- **Events.** Two or more distinct events that are independent of each other and strikingly similar occur within hours.

- **Parallels.** These two events share a long list of objective similarities. This list will be composed of specific, unlikely parallels surrounded by more general parallels. The list will tell an overall story and will capture something central about the two events.

- **Subject situation.** The CMPE is about a situation in your life that fits the overall story told by the parallels and is probably current, uncertain, unresolved, or at least needing confirmation. This situation is probably contained in one or more of the events, especially one that has the characteristics of an important event for you.

- **Interpretation.** The parallels and symbolic situation will together frame the subject situation in a certain way, a way that addresses your specific concern. The parallels do this by confirming aspects of the subject situation. The symbolic situation does this by telling a story that contains the truth about the subject situation.

This whole structure appears to be designed to get a message across to us. Through the *events* and *parallels*, the CMPE lets us know something out of the ordinary is going on, something non-random. In the *subject situation*, the CMPE highlights some situation of relevance to us. And then in the *interpretation*, the CMPE says something about that situation.

Of course, the entire thing hinges on that first part, that something non-random is going on here. It certainly looks that way. Yet can we be certain? After all, there is nothing conventionally impossible about the events involved. For instance, with the bucket brigade sign, it wasn't as if we were discussing forming a bucket brigade and then a bunch of buckets filled with water danced into the room on little feet. No, the events involved were quite ordinary. It was only their conjunction in time that was extraordinary. Couldn't we argue that that sort of conjunction may be unlikely, but should still be expected on rare occasions based on the laws of probability?

This argument can look reasonable when we are dealing with individual signs. However, one of the most remarkable things about signs is that they are hardly ever individual. It is unusual for me to have a sign that is not clearly connected with a network of other signs I have had. This interconnectedness is not an occasional characteristic of signs; it is part of their essential nature.

The extent of this interrelatedness is truly amazing, as I hope you will see in this chapter. It is something you never quite get used to. If one sign boggles the mind, making you wonder how this could be, then when you see that sign intimately connecting with a number of other signs, the boggle-factor increases exponentially. In my view, the consistency between different signs completely rules out the notion that this is all random. One could reasonably maintain that a single sign was just a fluke—a rare, but completely random conjunction of events. But when you see that this sign is a seamless part of a whole network of related signs, the randomness hypothesis becomes hopelessly untenable.

I have observed a number of different kinds of interconnectedness between signs. I'll briefly describe the kinds and then provide some examples.

Addressing the same situations

CMPEs "like" certain situations, and will return to them again and again. It would be nice if these situations were the ones in which we felt the greatest need for guidance. However, while being responsive to our needs, CMPEs also have a mind of their own. We can feel an intense need for guidance about a certain situation, yet CMPEs will consistently ignore it, while they continue to merrily comment on some other situation that we are not that concerned about. They have their favorites, and that, apparently, is that.

Conveying consistent messages

When CMPEs visit a situation again, you can count on the fact that the new message will agree with the previous one. It will probably not be the exact same message, but it will clearly be consistent. This is the most noticeable kind of connectedness between signs. A new sign will never say something that negates a previous sign.

Having a similar form

When you see two CMPEs say similar things about the same situation, if you look further, you will often notice the similarity doesn't stop with the *content* (the message) but rather continues into the *form*. For example, the events of the two signs may have similarities. The story told by the list of parallels may be similar. Even the symbols used may be the same. We'll see examples of all of this later.

The phenomenon of a linked series

Another fascinating phenomenon is where two or more related CMPEs occur close together in time. They can be anywhere from hours apart to a couple of weeks or more apart. But they are so clearly similar and so close together in time that you get the impression a single, larger message is coming through in two or three installments. I call these "linked series."

Similar signs occurring on the same dates

One of the features of signs that never ceases to amaze me is similar signs occurring on the same dates in different years. The story that opened the chapter, of course, was an example of this. Once I process a sign, I will look in my records for any related signs that occurred previously on that same date. Quite often, one will be there. I have looked through my records and found that one in every seven or eight signs will have a clear relationship with another sign that occurred on the exact same date in the previous five years. When it happens, it really hits you between the eyes, yet it happens quite regularly.

The two signs about this book

The interconnectedness of signs is so routine that we can see it in the two signs I recounted about this book. I am sure you remember "The How-To Component of this Book" from the end of Chapter 1. After a great deal of uncertainty, I had decided to include material in this book on how to work with and receive guidance from your own signs. As I wrote about that, I encountered a book that was primarily about how to receive guidance from the Holy Spirit. I concluded, "My signs book should definitely include a how-to component."

I'm sure you also remember "The Truth of Symbolism," the sign about symbolism that opened the previous chapter. Actually, it wasn't until I wrote about that in the last chapter that I noticed just how similar it was to the "how-to" sign. The two signs had been more than two years apart, and it had never occurred to me that they were similar. Yet they are, astonishingly so, as you can see from the following list of commonalities:

- There is an issue involving the writing of this book.

- This issue involves a particular subject that either Nicola or I are concerned will not be understood by readers (how-to instruction, symbolism).

- That concern is so strong that either she or I suggest that this subject should not be included in the book.

- Based on Nicola's advice, however, I decide to include the subject.

- I carry out this decision by writing a draft of part of the book, in which I say (or plan to say) that this subject will be included in the book, while also mentioning what provoked the caution about including it.

- Immediately after writing this, I read (or read about) another book.

- What I read in (or about) this other book is strikingly parallel to what I was just writing.

- As it turns out, this other book includes a subject that is extremely similar to the one I had finally decided to include.

- The relevant portion or aspect of the book is about how to receive wisdom for our lives from a supposedly divine source (Bible stories, Holy Spirit).

How could we possibly expect that two signs about the same book, separated by two years, would have this much in common? How does such a thing happen? Just to be clear, I have not gone back and edited the accounts of the two signs to exaggerate their similarity or even to draw out their similarity. The two signs really are this much alike.

This likeness spans three of the kinds of interconnectedness I mentioned earlier. First, it is an example of signs visiting the same basic situation again (my quandaries about the writing of this book). Second, it is an example of different signs having a consistent message (include that subject you were thinking about leaving out). Third, it is an example of different signs having a similar form, as the events of both signs involve the same basic plotline. You can see this identical plotline by reading down the list of commonalities above.

Further, something happens when you put these two signs together, something I haven't mentioned, yet is also routine. Together, the two signs project a larger message than either sign does by itself.

Look again at that list of commonalities above. Both stories are really about my concern that readers will not understand a certain topic. This, it turns out, is a major concern of mine about the book as a whole. I am trying to get across a new concept, one that, in my experience, takes time to understand. The signs have somehow managed to hone in on my most basic concern in the writing of this book—the fear it will not be understood.

What do they say about this? Rather than urging me to back off and leave out the thorny, hard-to-understand parts, they tell me to wade in. This is not to say they are blind to the risk. The sign about symbolism urges me to clarify the topic at length *because* of the risk of misunderstanding. Rather than brushing off the risk, then, the signs are simply saying, in the face of it, step forward, instead of back. That counsel can be applied to all kinds of issues in this book, simply because the temptation to step back exists, to varying degrees, across the board.

As I write this, I am just now realizing that the signs have extended this counsel beyond the boundaries of this book. The above paragraphs have just sparked my memory of another sign that gave this same advice in relation to another book. This other sign turns out to be astonishingly parallel to the two signs mentioned here, and so a brief account of it is in order.

I was about to write the conclusion to a book titled *Return to the Heart of God: The Practical Philosophy of 'A Course in Miracles.'* The book is my attempt to summarize the rather intricate and multilayered thought system of *A Course in Miracles.* As I pondered writing the conclusion, I found myself really wanting to express just how astounded I am at this thought system. I wondered, however, if that would meet the needs of my readers. In my experience, Course students want to hear about how the Course's ideas can help them in their lives. When I start talking about how amazing the Course as a whole is, they tend to glaze over. This issue was enough of a quandary that I was actually wondering if I could get away with not even writing a conclusion. I wanted to avoid the whole thing.

So I asked Nicola for her thoughts. She immediately felt that I shouldn't back off from saying what was in my heart to say, but that I should go even further in that direction. I should make the conclusion more personal, she said, sharing my own personal reactions when I stand before this thought system. This idea made me slightly nervous, but it felt like the right thing to do and I decided to follow her advice.

Less than an hour later I happened to pick up an article sent to me a few weeks before that was lying with other papers on my desk. It was written by Roger Walsh, a Professor of Psychiatry, Philosophy, Anthropology, and Religious Studies at UC Irvine. It was titled "The Perennial Wisdom of *A Course in Miracles.*" As I began to read it, I was immediately struck by how similar it was to what Nicola had just suggested. In the opening paragraphs, the author shared how, once he got over his resistance to the Course's Christian language,

I began to feel that this was a truly extraordinary work. During the past ten years I've studied it intently and my appreciation of it has continued to grow.

One of the hallmarks of a profound teaching is that when you go through it again, you find what philosophers call *"higher grades of significance."* This seems to happen each time I go through the Course. I'm now at the point where I feel it's on a par with any other material or discipline I've seen. Other people who are wiser than I agree. For example, Ken Wilber, who has read more widely in the world's psychologies and spiritual traditions than anyone I know, says the Course is on a level with anything he's run across. So I'm inclined to think that this document may be a spiritual masterpiece.

Here, then, was someone doing precisely what Nicola had advised me to do: reporting his personal reaction to the Course, relating how extraordinary he feels it is. As I read further, there were even more parallels between the article and what I planned to write. The events were definitely a sign, which was clearly confirming Nicola's idea about the conclusion to *Return to the Heart of God*.

This sign turned out to be extremely helpful. The conclusion I ended up writing has garnered more comments than the entire rest of the book (and it's a long book!). What interests me now, however, is just how similar this sign is to the other two signs. All three signs have the following things in common:

- I have an issue involving the writing of a book.
- The issue arises out of me feeling a disconnect between myself and my audience.
- This disconnect leads me (or Nicola) to wonder if I should leave out this part of the book.
- Based on Nicola's advice, however, I decide to include it and (in two

cases) go even more deeply into it.

- Immediately after either making or acting on this decision, I read (or read about) another author doing essentially the same thing I had decided to do. (In two cases, I fish this material seemingly at random out of the papers on my cluttered desk.)

- All of this constitutes a sign that tells me that, in facing this gap between me and my audience, rather than backing off, I need to step forward.

Notice how the issue has grown. Now it is no longer just about the how-to component or the symbolism topic in this book, or even just about this book. The signs are dissecting me as a writer. Somehow they grasped what I had only dimly felt, that as a writer I am always standing at the edge of a perceived canyon between me and my audience, tempted to back away in despair. Their advice is to do just the opposite. They want me to muster everything I have and jump that canyon.

I'm glad you could see this process, which more or less happened in front of your eyes, as this is a common sort of process for me. I had three signs, separated by years, that each qualified on its own and that I initially saw no link between. However, writing about them in this book prompted me to recognize their amazing similarities. What are the odds of three different signs all following the same detailed plotline? Finally, seeing their similarities caused me to see that they weren't separate pieces of advice. Rather, they were separate applications of a single global piece of advice. This advice is not the prosaic counsel that the three individual signs seemed to deliver. Rather, it is quite personal, not particularly comfortable, yet possibly priceless.

Nicola moving to America

We saw the same dates phenomenon at the beginning of the chapter. And we saw three of the other kinds of interconnectedness in the foregoing example. What we haven't seen is a linked series. The following example illustrates what a linked series is, and in the process actually contains all five kinds of interconnectedness I outlined above.

July 15, 2001

In summer 2001, Nicola moved here temporarily from England to do spiritual healing for the Circle of Atonement. Offering healing was an important first for us and we were wondering how to publicize Nicola's work so she would get clients. On July 15, a friend of ours suggested a method: trying to get articles about Nicola's healing published in various local periodicals. That same day, Nicola received an e-mail containing the apparent news that this idea had, in essence, already been carried out. A friend of hers from England wrote:

> I read an amazing article in *The Independent on Sunday* magazine about 2/3 weeks back about the centre in Sedona. It mentioned an English woman who had recently moved out there, using aromatherapy and massage to help guests at the centre find peace and spiritual rejuvenation. Was this you, I wonder...?
>
> In any case, it was a very, very good piece and I thought that it would attract a lot of favourable interest in the centre for all the work that was being done there.

We had no idea what she was talking about. Our small center had, to our knowledge, not been featured in any newspaper, let alone one all the way across the Atlantic. However, the parallels with our friend's idea for publicizing Nicola's healing were unmistakable. In both cases, an English woman who has moved to Sedona, Arizona is doing alternative healing at a center there. This is being written about in a periodical, and this attracts "favourable interest" in her work. It was an obvious sign, one that needed no further interpretation.

July 30, 2001

Two weeks later, on July 30, a sequel occurred. In event 1, we received a transcript of a talk Nicola had given on her journey as a healer. A year earlier, Nicola had visited Sedona to give this talk and offer healing sessions.

She was so well-received that this influenced our decision to try to get her here on a more permanent basis. Now that she *was* here, we had asked a friend to type up the transcript as a way to publicize her healing. This transcript had now arrived.

In event 2, we received a number of responses to an announcement we had recently posted on our website about Nicola beginning healing at the Circle.

These two events didn't make for a sign. However, that same day event 3 happened. We received an e-mail in which another *Course in Miracles* center was publicizing the arrival of a spiritual healer to do healing work. It said,

> After witnessing the incredible healings that occurred during his June visit, we are pleased to announce the return of the Brazilian spiritual healer, Rubens Faria/Dr. Fritz to the Miracles Healing Center.

This was followed by the story of the "incredible healings" that had happened on Dr. Fritz's first visit, along with testimonials from those healed.

You might expect spiritual healing would be quite common in centers devoted to *A Course in Miracles*, yet oddly enough, it is actually extremely rare. This made the parallels from that day's events quite striking: There is a spiritual healer from a distant country (England, Brazil) who has been brought back to a *Course in Miracles* center in the U.S. after the healer's first visit there was very well-received. The center then announces this return visit via e-mail and also publicizes it with a written report from the healer's first visit.

These parallels were already enough for a CMPE. Yet before the day was over, a fourth event occurred. That day I took Nicola to the local Motor Vehicles Division to get her American driver's license. There, we ran into an acquaintance named Kate, who was there to change her address on her driver's license, since she had recently moved. Both Kate and Nicola were from the south of England, and so the two of them got to chatting. Kate, it turns out, was doing alternative healing, specifically, massage, at the local

Enchantment resort, in their "Mii Amo" spa, which aimed to renew the physical, emotional, and spiritual well-being of those who came.

The highly coincidental encounter with Kate was littered with parallels. Here we had two women who had moved to Sedona from the south of England. Both were here doing alternative healing work at a local center or spa dedicated to spiritual renewal. Both had just relocated and, as a result, one was getting a new license and the other was getting a change of address on her license. It was as if they were mirror images of each other.

So here we had a four-event CMPE. In it, both Dr. Fritz and Kate functioned as symbols for Nicola. Both symbolically depicted Nicola coming here from a distant country to do healing for the Circle of Atonement. The Dr. Fritz symbol emphasized publicizing Nicola's healing, while the Kate symbol emphasized Nicola's relocation here.

We, of course, immediately saw a relationship between this new sign and the earlier July 15 one. Both signs were talking about Nicola moving here to do healing and about the need to publicize that healing. What had us especially mesmerized, however, was that both used the symbol of an English woman who had moved to Sedona and was doing alternative healing at a center devoted to spiritual renewal. In the July 15 sign, she was the mystery woman in the magazine article; in the July 30 sign, she was Kate. Two signs using such similar symbols struck us as wildly improbable.

August 2, 2001

Just three days later, on August 2, we had a stunning conclusion to the series. Based on a yearly reading schedule for *A Course in Miracles*, I was studying a section titled "The Little Garden." This section contains a beautiful metaphor of a little garden arising in a barren desert. This garden is a holy place. To its green oasis come those who have been lost in the desert, thirsting for living water. There, they find rest and rejuvenation, and though they came alone, they leave with a friend. In this metaphor, the desert symbolizes the world, a place deprived of the water of life-giving love. And the garden symbolizes someone who has allowed real love into his or her mind. This person's loving presence now becomes an oasis where people take refuge, to recover from a lifetime of wandering under the scorching glare of hate.

That same day, the article that was part of the July 15 sign arrived in the mail. We were sure, of course, that Nicola wasn't the healer in the article, but we had to see it anyway, so we asked her friend to send it. Once it arrived, we saw that this article did indeed describe a place here in Sedona. It was a renowned spa that was spoken of as an oasis in the desert (it topped the article's list of "Oasis Places"). It was also described as a holy place, "a sacred spot you must approach with silent reverence." People briefly leave their lives and come there, almost on pilgrimages, seeking rejuvenation of mind, body, and spirit. And that is just what the woman who wrote the article appears to have found. She came with her sister, and when they left, she says, "I check the bags under my eyes...and for the first time in ages, they are gone. My sister has shed years; she looks as if she's been on sabbatical." Along the way, she describes being given the spa's signature treatment, designed to release spiritual "negativity," by a tall young woman who was originally from England.

The article was so parallel with the "Little Garden" section that its arrival made for yet another sign. Both spoke of an oasis in the desert, a holy place, where people visit in order to find spiritual renewal. And both speak of that garden's rejuvenating effects flowing from a particular person (in the "Little Garden" section, the reader was called to become this person; in the magazine article, it was the English healer). In the sign, this place clearly symbolized the Circle of Atonement and the healer symbolized Nicola. The sign was saying, in other words, that the Circle should become an oasis in the desert, where people come to find spiritual healing and rejuvenation, and that Nicola should be a specific agent of that.

Though having a third sign in the series was impressive, what really stunned us was something else. As we read, we realized that the spa in this article was the one Kate worked at—Mii Amo at the Enchantment Resort. We also realized—and here is where our jaws dropped—that the massage therapist in the article must be Kate herself. We immediately called Kate and she confirmed that, yes, it was her!

As you can imagine, we were absolutely floored. Here were three linked signs, occurring over the space of eighteen days. All three spoke of Nicola coming to the Circle of Atonement to do spiritual healing, and *all three* (it turned out) used Kate as a symbol for that. News of Kate's work at Mii Amo had shown up first in the form of hearing about the article, then in the form of running into Kate in town, and finally in the form of getting the article in the mail. Each time this news showed up, it was accompanied by parallel events that made for a sign, a sign that used Kate as a symbol for Nicola.

We found this truly mind-boggling. We couldn't stop speculating about how something like this gets arranged. What is the mechanism behind it? Alternatively, what are the odds of all this occurring by chance? It seemed inconceivable. It felt impossible to not see some kind of guiding hand in all this.

A similar linked series from the year before

We had an additional reason to be amazed at this linked series of CMPEs. A year earlier, in 2000, when Nicola had first visited Sedona, we experienced another linked series of signs. Unbelievably, this series had occurred on the exact same dates: July 15, July 30, and August 2!

Here are excerpts from my original interpretations of those three signs. Every word of these interpretations was written a year before the 2001 signs I related above:

> *July 15*: "The simple message I got from this sign is that we [the Circle] are supposed to manifest the pattern I wrote about in that social vision article [which was centered on the 'little garden' concept in *A Course in Miracles*]…inviting Course students from all over to come and take retreats here and experience our support system."

> *July 30 (a massive seven-event sign)*: "The Circle as it now stands is like a garden that has been carefully prepared for her [Nicola] to come into it and find a home.…Her presence there will invite new people into the garden, people who specifically need the healing gifts that she offers. This, in fact, reflects the whole nature of what the Circle is meant to be. It is meant to be

a garden in the desert [a reference to the 'little garden'], which invites into it all those who are weary of a world that is devoid of life-sustaining love. There, they find healing, and because of their presence, the garden expands."

August 2: "In your trip to Sedona you [Nicola] accepted your role. You accepted the calling you have to work with the Circle and the contribution you have to make to it as a healer."

These CMPEs, as you can see, were not only on the same dates as the 2001 linked series, but they also focused on the *same themes.* Both series speak of Nicola moving to Sedona to do healing at the Circle, and both speak of the Circle embodying the "little garden" image in *A Course in Miracles.* Just as in 2001 Mii Amo had repeatedly shown up as the "little garden" symbol, so in 2000 this role was filled by a book called *Gardens from the Sand.* In this book (written by a *Course in Miracles* student), a man grows a "little garden" in the desert, to which people flock from distant places. This book had shown up in two of the signs.

Now you know the full reason we were so astonished by the linked series of 2001. We had seen it all before. Two series of signs, each announcing the same set of themes and each occurring in adjacent years on the *exact same three dates.* How on earth does something like that happen?

Could it happen again?

The first series had been in 2000, and the second in 2001. By summer 2003, the situation the signs had spoken of had advanced considerably. Nicola had returned to England the previous year to deal with her marriage, and she was now in the process of ending it, which was to be followed by a permanent move to America. This move, of course, was the very situation the earlier signs had spoken of.

Then a sign about this process occurred on July 15. This quite naturally caused us to wonder if we were in for yet another linked series on the same three dates. Each time we talked about this possibility over the next two weeks, we would say, "That would be amazing, but honestly—how could it happen again?" Then a sign happened on July 30 that was intimately related to the July 15 sign. That was two out of three. Finally, a third sign occurred on August 2, one that was closely linked to the first two. It *had* happened again.

(I should add that we are absolute sticklers for not "bringing on" signs. When an important sign date rolls around, we try not to mention it until the day is over, and we especially try to not have it influence what we do on that day.)

These signs were extremely personal, which is why I'm not sharing their details. The Circle only showed up in one of the signs, and the "little garden" concept didn't show up at all. But this series *was* about Nicola moving here, just as the other two series were, and it did happen on the same exact three dates. It was clearly number three in what we might call *a linked series of linked series*.

As I said earlier, these three linked series display all five of the kinds of interconnectedness I listed at the beginning of the chapter:

- **Same situation.** All three series spoke to the issue of Nicola moving to America. This was a favorite topic for the signs until she actually did move, three weeks after the final August 2 sign.

- **Consistent messages.** The group of signs as a whole affirmed that Nicola should move here to take her place in the Circle of Atonement, which would become like the "little garden" in *A Course in Miracles*.

- **Similar form.** The "similar form" here was primarily the recurring symbol of a healer in residence at an oasis in the desert (five signs). This was sometimes the healing person in the "little garden" in the Course (two signs), sometimes the man in the little garden in *Gardens from the Sand* (two signs), and sometimes Kate doing healing work at Mii Amo (three signs).

- **Linked series.** There were, of course, *three* linked series, each consisting of three related CMPEs occurring over a two and a half-week period.

- **Same dates.** Most remarkable of all, in three different, nearly consecutive years there were signs on July 15, July 30, and August 2 about Nicola moving here.

All of this interrelatedness, of course, gives the overwhelming impression that these nine signs were not connected by mere random chance. You get the distinct feeling that whatever organizing principle was at work in one sign was equally at work in them all. The nine signs begin to look like different aspects of a single overall event.

This obviously makes the whole thing immeasurably more difficult to explain away as chance. Now, you have to explain away, not just a single CMPE, but an entire network of nine closely related CMPEs. With one sign, you might be able to reasonably imagine that it was just a fluke, just a case of monkeys happening, *this time*, to randomly type a coherent sentence. Yet as you stand before a highly organized network of nine signs (especially if they all happened to you), your mind is involuntarily dragged toward the raw acknowledgment that this cannot—simply *cannot*—be monkeys randomly banging on typewriters. You feel as if you are standing before a phenomenon as orderly as the stars wheeling overhead, a force that can organize the random events of your life into something as intelligent as a musical score.

To use another analogy of animal behavior, imagine that your dog happened to bark out a word in Morse code. You would probably dismiss it as chance—a wild improbability, but still chance. But imagine that it happened repeatedly, and that the words, when added together, actually formed a sentence (such as, "I prefer the other dog food"). What would happen then to your perception of this situation? Would you still be able to dismiss it as mere chance?

Conclusion

The interrelatedness of CMPEs is crucial in establishing that we are dealing with a genuine phenomenon and not a series of random accidents. Unfortunately, this brief chapter cannot begin to convey just how interconnected different CMPEs really are. For instance, with each of the situations we looked at here (the Circle's fundraising, the writing of this book, my writing in general, Nicola moving here, the Circle becoming a "little garden" in the desert), there are many more signs than what I have shared, and all of them interlock with those that I have. Indeed, when you pull together all the signs about any one of these situations, they form a jigsaw puzzle that contains a larger vision of that situation, larger than what any one sign expressed. We saw this very thing with the signs about my writing.

Yet the interrelatedness doesn't stop there, for none of these situations is an island. Each one, of course, overlaps with other situations in my life, and from what I can see, the *signs* about these situations fully reflect this overlap. It's as if the overall vision the signs express about any one of my situations is really just a single piece of a much bigger puzzle—the larger vision they convey about my life as a whole.

Yet, as you might imagine, it doesn't stop there, for obviously my life overlaps with the lives of others, and in my experience, the signs about those others fit masterfully with the signs about me. Often, for example, a single sign will say something about two or more people. In such cases, each person in that sign will show up "in character"—in a way that is consistent with what previous signs have said about that person. It's quite impressive when you see it (and we'll see examples later). From this perspective, the signs' overall vision of my life is really just a single piece of a larger puzzle, a puzzle that also includes the lives around me.

Of course, that's as far as I can see right now. Though I have hundreds of CMPEs in my logs, almost all of them are about my life and the lives of people I know. For now, that's as far as my horizon goes. But if all I can see is clockwork-like consistency all the way to that horizon, why should I assume it stops there? Why should I assume it suddenly drops over the edge like some sailing ship before Columbus? Why shouldn't I assume it keeps going?

And yet, if it *does*, if it does keep going, think about that. Think what that would mean. It would mean that all CMPEs, the world over, are tiny pieces of a single colossal puzzle, a single plan for the world as a whole.

If one day a discipline arose composed of researchers from around the world, who through painstaking research verified that this is quite likely the case, that this single global puzzle most likely exists, what would that do to our picture of things? What would that do to our understanding of the nature of reality and the purpose of life?

Chapter 8
Can Signs Predict the Future?

The Dead Sea Scrolls

In October 1991, I had just received a new book about Helen Schucman, the woman who "scribed" *A Course in Miracles* by taking down the words of an inner voice. Because I have an interest in the Dead Sea Scrolls, the first thing I read in this book was an experience Helen had while visiting Qumran, the ruins of the community in Israel whose scribes produced the Dead Sea Scrolls 2,000 years ago.

In this story, Helen is standing in front of one of the caves where the scrolls had been discovered and immediately recognizes this cave. She bursts into tears and says this is the exact cave she had seen in a vision eight years earlier, a vision in which she entered a cave and discovered an ancient scroll. Visibly moved, she exclaims that this is the holiest place on earth. Then she has the strange sense that she had actually been a member of the Qumran community (although she was skeptical about past lives). The story made me wonder if she hadn't been a scribe there, and that if, as scribe of the Course, she wasn't repeating a role she had played in ancient times.

The next day, October 2, was when the CMPE occurred. While in the supermarket, the latest edition of *U.S. News* caught my eye, again because of my interest in the Dead Sea Scrolls. Its cover story was about the dramatic release to the public of previously unpublished scrolls.

The article said the scrolls had initially generated such excitement because they "offered new insights into the nature of the Bible and provided tantalizing glimpses into the turbulent times that gave birth to Christianity and modern Judaism." Yet even though they had been discovered in the 40's and 50's, nearly half of the scrolls were still unpublished. For forty years they had remained the exclusive possession of a small team of scholars, who had been carefully assembling and translating the fragments, while other scholars around the world were perennially kept in the dark. This had become an "academic scandal par excellence," as one famous scholar noted. There were even suggestions th at certain scrolls were being suppressed because they might prove damaging to traditional religious beliefs. This deadlock, however, had now dramatically broken loose:

> Last week, in a surprise move, a private California research library that holds one of just four complete photographic sets of the scroll collection opened its vaults and began granting access to the scroll photographs to all qualified scholars....[This] came just two weeks after the Biblical Archaeology Society, which has led a decades-long crusade to "liberate" the scrolls, released a computerized reconstruction of some of the unpublished material derived from an official con- cordance.

I returned home and continued reading the new book on Helen Schucman. Its author was part of a very small circle that had formed around Helen while she was alive, and he had access to material she had scribed that was not included in *A Course in Miracles*. His book thus contained thousands of words of this scribed material that the public had never seen, or even knew existed. And this new material, at least in my eyes, threw new light onto the origins of *A Course in Miracles*, as well as onto its teaching. Why had it been kept private, I wondered?

In the midst of this discovery, I received a phone call from a friend who was reading the same book. He drew my attention to a particular piece of this new material, which was about the resurrection of Jesus. He pointed out to me that although the author of the book included this material, he also tried to discount it. It didn't agree with his view of the resurrection and he suggested that in this case, Helen's hearing (of the inner voice) had been distorted by her own fears.

This material on the resurrection had been known to me, but I also knew that this same author had disouraged others (myself included) from publishing it. Now I suspected I knew why—because he considered it discordant with the larger teaching of the Course, as he interpreted that teaching. As my conversation with my friend ended, I noticed this guidance had been taken down on this very day fifteen years earlier— October 2, 1976.

There were so many parallels between the magazine article and the phone conversation that it had to be a CMPE. There is scripture-like material produced by "scribes" (the Dead Sea Scrolls, the unpublished Course material). These scribes were either members of the Qumran community or felt they may have been a member in the past (as I had discovered about Helen the previous day). This material had the potential to throw crucial light on a book considered by some to be scripture (the Bible, the Course) and on the beginnings of a particular religious/spiritual tradition (Christianity, modern Judaism, the Course tradition). It had long been the exclusive property of a small group, who had kept it secret from colleagues and the public. There is the suggestion that they did this because it said things they didn't want said. But now, at long last, it was being published. There were just too many parallels for the whole thing to be chance.

This CMPE captivated me, but what did it mean? It was clearly granting significance to the release of this hitherto-unpublished Course material. Yet I felt there was more to it. The situation with the Dead Sea Scrolls was the symbol, the authoritative commentary. And what did it show? It showed a group of individuals who were so reluctant to release the material they held that, as long as it was up to them, that material didn't get released—at least not completely. It only came out in its entirety when other people took matters into their own hands. This symbol had a real impact on me. I felt sure the sign was saying there was more material Helen scribed that was still being kept secret.

This idea captivated me. Therefore, when some months later I visited someone from that original circle around Helen, I had to check it out. My first question was if there were still more material of Helen's being held back. He said there wasn't, aside from a very small amount about two minor topics (which he declined to let me see). I was surprised, but since this man had intimate knowledge of these materials, I concluded I must have misread the sign. I put the whole thing behind me.

But that wasn't the end. Eight years later, in the year 2000, someone (in a move of questionable legality) released over the Internet an earlier, less-edited version of *A Course in Miracles*, which contained an additional 30 pages of material, much of it never seen before. Several months after that, an even earlier version was released, with 60 additional pages of "new" material. So there *had* been more unpublished scribal material from Helen. Whether intentionally or unintentionally, I had been misinformed.

When these events played out, I was stunned. I felt like one of those people who had dreamt about a plane crash and then saw it on TV. In both the 1991 Dead Sea Scrolls sign and the events in 2000 the same thing happened: "Scribed" material had for decades been kept under wraps by the original circle until someone else took it into their own hands to release it to the world. Indeed, in both cases, there had been two such releases. Clearly, my original interpretation had proved entirely correct.

This dramatic confirmation left me wondering: How on earth did that sign know? How did it know the situation with the Course would end up spookily mirroring the "guerrilla" release of the Dead Sea Scrolls—eight years before it happened?

All of us want to know the future. Sometimes this is mere idle curiosity, which, even if satisfied, would not actually add anything to our lives. Sometimes, though, it is more than that. Every action we take rests on prediction of what lies in the future, even if it's only prediction of what will happen if this action is carried out. In this case, desire to know the future is more than idle curiosity. It is practical necessity.

How well do CMPEs perform in predicting the future? It would be exciting if they showed real skill in this area, for the fact is that all of our crystal balls—from complex calculations to literal crystal balls—are notoriously inaccurate. There was a memorable commercial in which a man complained, "It is the year 2000, but where are the flying cars?" We could use a crystal ball that really worked.

I don't receive very many signs that are pure predictions. Most predict things will work out *if* I follow a particular course of action. If things then don't work out, I am left wondering if the fault lay in the signs or in myself—in my shortcomings in following their advice. However, the small number of CMPEs that have predicted future conditions beyond my control seem to me to have been impressively accurate. The following stories will give you a flavor of what I mean.

Signs about the copyright on a contemporary spiritual classic

The longest string of predictive CMPEs I have experienced has been about the copyright situation around *A Course in Miracles*, a drama that lasted many years and whose twists and turns kept all of us guessing— except the signs.

A number of authors, including myself, write books based on *A Course in Miracles*. For these authors the ability to quote from the Course is obviously a key issue. For the first fifteen or so years after the Course was published in 1976, authors were able to quote freely. However, this eventually changed, resulting in an intense community-wide controversy, lasting roughly from 1999 to 2003, which included four lawsuits and a challenge to the copyright on the Course itself. Somehow, the signs seemed to know that this controversy was coming, as well as how it would end.

In fact, the very first sign I had about the copyright controversy was the Dead Sea Scrolls sign I related above. The release of those two earlier versions of *A Course in Miracles* was actually a direct result of the copyright controversy. However, the sign was so far ahead of its time that I didn't realize until years later that it was about that controversy. In my awareness, the first sign about the copyright situation came the following year.

A sign of things to come

In 1992, I was attending a *Course in Miracles* conference on the East Coast. There, I was talking with another Course teacher about the issue of permission to quote from the Course. He told me the organization that owned the Course's copyright was quite strict and protective in its attitude, even though its public policy was very permissive. I had never heard this and didn't know what to make of his statements.

Yet on this same day, somewhere around the same time, the head of that very organization called my home in Arizona and left a message. She said the policy on permission to quote was tightening, and that, because of this, a project I was working on—an audio tape of various Course passages on forgiveness—was being denied permission. This was a dramatic departure; I had never heard of a project being denied permission to quote.

The two conversations that day clearly added up to a CMPE, one that gave me an ominous feeling. It said there was something significant about this tightening in the Course's copyright policy, something that would affect my work. I had no idea how true that would prove to be.

The situation heats up

Over the next few years, the policy on permission to quote from *A Course in Miracles* continued to tighten, until no more than 5% of a book's word count could consist of Course quotes. For those of us writing commentary strictly about the Course, being able to quote only two lines per page was simply not workable.

On September 4, 1996, I made a trip to California to visit with the head of the organization that owned the copyright. I had received a letter from her that implied legal action if the Circle didn't agree to quote within narrow boundaries. Rather than accept that scenario, I planned to present a proposal I felt could potentially solve things. My proposal was that there be *narrower* permission for "Course-inspired" writers who are only drawing partly on the Course, and *broader* permission for "Course specific" writers who write only about the Course. This included permission both to quote and to use the Course's now-trademarked title.

I was quite hopeful about this visit. Yet as I was preparing to leave, I had another one of those ominous signs. A friend of mine was currently helping to found a Waldorf charter school in the area. Waldorf is an educational movement founded by the philosopher Rudolf Steiner in the 1920's. My friend, however, had just heard from Waldorf headquarters that the new school was being denied permission to use the Waldorf name. Because the new school would receive state funds, the separation of church and state required it to leave out the spiritual elements in the Waldorf philosophy. The parent organization felt they had granted too much permission to schools like this, and as a result the purity of the Waldorf philosophy was being compromised. Further, a controversy had flared up in some states around state-funded Waldorf charter schools, specifically because of their quasi-religious elements. It was time, headquarters felt, to regain control they had given away.

While talking with my friend about this, I received a call from a fellow Course student. Knowing nothing about the meeting I was about to have, he called to voice suspicions about the copyright holder of the Course. He suspected a recent decision of theirs was just a move to strengthen their copyright, in response to a lawsuit that had just challenged the copyright (the first of the copyright suits). He had even heard a rumor (which was not true) that they had brought suit against the Circle. He believed they felt they had given away too much control, and now they were trying to reel it back in.

These two conversations felt strangely similar. In both cases, there is the parent organization of a spiritual movement trying to regain control they gave away. They are trying to reclaim their spiritual product and take it back out of the hands of those who, in their view, might dilute it. This involves intellectual property—trademark and/or copyright. As a result of all this, it is said that they are denying permission to or taking action against a smaller organization in Sedona, Arizona.

It was clearly a negative sign, which dashed my hopes for the next day's meeting. The meeting, however, went surprisingly well. The head of the board said my proposal brought things back to a needed balance. She asked my lawyer to get in touch with their lawyer to finalize things. The CMPE had apparently been wrong.

Yet the proposal was never finalized. I tried several times to reenergize the process, but it just never went anywhere. Indeed, subsequent events, as you will see, reflected everything the sign had said.

Abandoning the baby

A year later, I sought the copyright holder's permission to quote from the

Course in a book that was meant to be my major statement on *A Course in Miracles*. I considered this my big break, as a high-profile literary agent believed he could sell this book to a major publisher. He just needed me to obtain permission to quote from the Course. I told him this wouldn't be a problem, as I had an understanding with the copyright holder (my earlier proposal). Yet an entire frustrating year then passed without me receiving a decision from the copyright holder.

Then, on February 22, 1999, I had a long phone conversation with the head of the copyright-holding organization (the person I had pitched my proposal to). I shared with her my impression that the decision about my book was no longer in the hands of her and her board, but had been placed in the hands of a particular man on her board. If this was true, it was bad news for me. Whereas she had a strong investment in seeing the Course get out to the world (and my book—being published by a major publisher— would be an instance of that), this man was perhaps the one person on earth who had reason to *not* want my book to be published. He was a fellow teacher of the Course whose interpretation was quite different than mine. Surely, I said to her, this decision had not been taken out of her hands and placed in his. I was shocked to hear her confirm that, yes, this was in fact what had happened.

While I was talking to her, a friend walked in and wanted to talk to me. After waiting until I was done, this friend then proceeded to tell me about a personal situation that was eerily parallel to the one I had just been discussing. In this situation, a wife was surrendering to her former husband a crucial decision about their child's life in the world, a decision the former husband was not well-equipped to make. The more I talked with my friend, the more I felt I was having the same conversation I had just had. It was a definite CMPE.

In a last-ditch effort to change the mind of the head of the Course organization, I sat down to write her a letter. I told her the story of my second conversation, and said that I felt it was given to me as a kind of symbol to illuminate my conversation with her. Using its imagery, I then said,

If I may be so bold, it seems to me that your real baby is seeing that the Course does not stay penned up in a closet, but gets out there to the world. If that in fact is your baby, then my book is a part of your baby—it is a clear case of the Course either being kept in a closet or let out of that closet. Could it be that you have abandoned that baby to a father [the other teacher mentioned above] who does not know how to take care of it?

I heard from her about two weeks later. She began the conversation by saying she found my letter "so insightful" because of what she was about to tell me. Then she told me her organization had formally handed over the copyright on *A Course in Miracles* to that other teacher's organization. This, she explained, was why my book's permission to quote had been placed in his hands. A few days later, I received a letter from him denying me permission to quote from the Course in my book.

In the midst of feeling as if the rug had been pulled out from under me—my book was now stopped in its tracks—I noted that the sign had seen more deeply than I could have realized. In my interpretation, I had talked about abandoning "the baby to a father who does not know how to take care of it." I believed that the "baby" being abandoned was the process of the Course reaching the world. In hindsight, I had the feeling the signs knew that what was being abandoned was more fundamental; it was ownership of the Course itself.

The Course copyright controversy erupts

At this point, all hell broke loose in the Course community as the new copyright holder policed the usage of Course quotations and title to an unheard of degree. A much stricter copyright policy was immediately instituted. Anonymous communications were sent to teachers, churches, and centers throughout the Course community, threatening legal action. Under threats from lawyers, websites were removed by their servers and Internet discussion groups shut down. Within about a year, four lawsuits around the copyright were in process, one of them with my organization, the Circle of Atonement.

Yet oddly enough, just at this lowest point the CMPEs changed their tune. Their message had been consistently dark for eight years now, even though for most of that time things hadn't looked all that bad. Yet now that the storm clouds they had spoken of were actually overhead, the signs started foretelling a future in which those clouds would be gone for good.

On September 29 of that year (1999), two people independently shared with me astrology readings they believed were about me, though neither one had been done for me. Rather strikingly, both readings acknowledged the blockages to publishing around the Course and said that these would be removed. The second one—from an astrologer who was not even aware of the Course itself, let alone the copyright controversy—was especially interesting. It said a particular man was responsible for the publishing blockages and promised that when they were resolved, the Course would be able to reach out to the world like never before. My interpretation focused on that second reading, saying, "The reading is right in saying that it will all get resolved and perhaps it is right in saying the Course will be able to be promoted and to spread like never before."

"The Shining Stranger"

On May 18, 2001, we found ourselves in arbitration with the new copyright holders. A year earlier, we had reached a mediated agreement with them, but when we tried to implement the agreement, things broke down, with the result that publishing new materials became extremely difficult for us. The arbitration, then, was our attempt to free ourselves to do our work.

The day I was at the arbitration, my colleague Greg had a particularly prescient CMPE. Someone asked him to put a link in our website to a story titled "The Shining Stranger." It was a fictional story about a mysterious woman who visits *Course in Miracles* groups and tells them of a secret plan to free the Course from the shackles of the copyright. First, the "stranger" summarized the current state of affairs: "Books are suppressed and dissident voices are persecuted. Scholarship has all but stopped; The Course Community is in decline and disarray." Then she guaranteed all this will change: "*A Course in Miracles* will be in the public domain....When this happens, we expect a renaissance, a revival of interest in its message." The story ended as the "shining stranger" promised that "the long, dark night would soon be over. And help was on its way."

That evening, Greg watched a movie on television called *Dark City*. It is about one man who, through a secret plan, frees his fellow human beings from the shackles of oppressive aliens called "the Strangers." The aliens, and the humans they control, live in a city that is in perpetual night. At the end, the hero of the story frees his fellow humans and brings daylight to the city. The long dark night is finally over, just as in "The Shining Stranger" story.

The parallelism between *Dark City* and "The Shining Stranger," along with their convergence on the day of our arbitration, convinced Greg this was a sign. Here is his interpretation:

> Right now, the Course is in bondage....But it will not always be this way. Help is on the way; the Course will be freed. The oppression will end; the light will come....Regardless of what happens at the arbitration, we needn't worry. All will be well, and we will be freed in due time.

Now two signs had said that the Course would be freed from its bondage. The second one was especially clear in saying that the copyright itself would go away. This was a gutsy prediction—and one that I frankly doubted. Only one remaining lawsuit would challenge the copyright in court, but the judge by this point had already ruled against twelve of the thirteen arguments brought against the copyright. Legal experts were saying the copyright would most likely stand. Things did not look good for those who wanted the judge to void the copyright.

The copyright is voided

Yet that is exactly what happened. On October 24, 2003, Judge Robert W. Sweet of the Southern District Court of New York found that the Course was distributed prior to publication and, as a result, ruled that its copyright was invalid. Seven months later, the judge's order went into effect and the copyright on *A Course in Miracles* passed away for good.

Looking back at the copyright signs, the overwhelming impression I get is that *they knew.* They often went against appearances and against my own assessments, but again and again they proved correct. When things didn't seem so bad—and even when nothing had yet happened—they knew there were dark days ahead. And when those dark days arrived, they knew that, against the odds, the Course would be freed from its constraints.

While making this string of successful predictions, the signs were also painting an overall vision of the situation. In this vision, the Course was being cooped up by its owners, but instead, matters needed to be taken out of their hands so the Course could be free to reach the world. Remarkably, this basic theme was announced in the very first sign (the Dead Sea Scrolls sign) and was clearly visible in almost every sign thereafter.

Along the way, the signs registered some strong disagreement with the copyright holders of the Course, which makes this a difficult and delicate story to tell. Yet that disagreement ended up being shared by the vast majority of observers, both inside the Course community and outside. The only difference is that the signs began sounding the alarm long before anyone else caught even a whiff of smoke.

The CMPEs are still speaking to this situation and still doing so in the exact same vein. For they had predicted (a number of times, actually) that when the Course is finally free, it "will be able to be promoted and to spread like never before." Now that it *is* free, this appears to be happening. The process is only in its very beginning stages, but as it unfolds, the signs are there, flagging key developments.

For example, the Circle finally published that book of mine that had been stopped by the copyright controversy all those years ago (now called *Return to the Heart of God*). Its release was therefore a great symbol of what is possible now that the copyright is gone. As publication date approached, we designed an e-mail announcement of the book, complete with photo of the cover, to send to our list. It would be the first word we had breathed of the book. When we finally sent this announcement out, we received *another* e-mail announcement from *another* Course center, sent just two minutes before. It, too, was an announcement of new products, complete with photos of their covers. Its opening words were "The new *A Course in Miracles* products keep coming." The message then displayed several products that had just recently come out (including portions of those two earlier versions released in 2000), all made possible by the passing away of the copyright.

Signs about a baby

I experienced another string of predictive signs about the first child I had with Nicola. I mentioned in Chapter 2 that a CMPE had successfully predicted the sex of my first child, Adam. The same thing then happened again three years later when my second child, Anna, was born. In both cases, there had been a clear sign that portrayed the child as either a boy or a girl. In both cases, the sex of the child was unknown by ordinary means until the moment of birth. And in both cases, the signs were correct.

I experienced a third installment of this with my third child, Miranda, who, as you know by now, I had with Nicola. This time, however, there wasn't just one CMPE, but rather a series of sixteen, which began nearly six years before Miranda was born. I won't be going into detail about the individual signs, because some of them were very personal and some were very complex (the most important sign included a whopping six events). However, I will quote my interpretations, which were written down well before the birth—in some cases, years before.

The CMPEs about Miranda began in December 1999. From the beginning, they said Nicola would have a child and portrayed that child as a girl. By summer 2001, there had been four such signs. I examined all these together and penned this conclusion: "The baby will be the extension of you [Nicola]. It will therefore be a girl who inherits much of who you are as a person."

Finally, in November 2004, Nicola—who by now was in America with me—got pregnant. Signs then continued to come, repeating and expanding on the themes already established. Oddly, the signs that came after conception talked in exactly the same way as the ones from five years before. It was as if, from their perspective, nothing had changed.

First, they continued to portray the child as a girl. Soon we had a total of four signs (two from before conception, two from after) that seemed to explicitly predict the child would be female. Not only that, throughout the sixteen CMPEs, there had been ten different children used as symbols of our baby. Remarkably, nine out of these ten were girls!

Second, the signs continued to place the "girl" prediction in a larger context, in which the infant would inherit Nicola's sex because it would inherit Nicola's nature in general. As I had written to Nicola earlier, it would inherit "much of who you are as a person."

I wanted to get this whole picture down on paper before the birth. So six weeks ahead of time, I summarized what these sixteen signs had said. Here is what I wrote:

The nature of the baby

The keynote of the baby is that it is an extension of Nicola. Nicola passes on who she is to the baby. Nicola will pass on her sex, so that the baby will be a girl. She will pass on her musical ability, so that the baby will have that ability as well. And she will pass on her personality, so that the baby will be similar to her as a person, possibly having her qualities of being kind, friendly, intelligent, and hard-working. (July 16, 2005)

At this point, we didn't know the baby's sex, as Nicola wanted to do it the old-fashioned way. She wanted the excitement of her and everyone else finding out at the moment of birth. This made the baby's sex a huge test of the signs for us. They had made a definite, consistent prediction that would unambiguously prove either right or wrong.

If it was right, it would be mildly impressive, in that it would be the third straight successful prediction of one of my children's sex. If it was wrong, however, it would be devastating for the signs. At this point, the baby was right there inside Nicola's body. Its sex was already fixed and could be easily observed by medical instruments. Strictly speaking, this was no longer *prediction*. If the signs couldn't peer a couple of inches inside Nicola's belly, how all-seeing could they be?

It all came down to the moment of the birth. We (well, mainly Nicola) had to endure thirty-three hours of labor, but when the baby finally emerged, I was able to see her as she came out. I immediately turned and whispered to Nicola, "It's a girl!" She has told me many times that she will never forget me saying that.

What about the rest of the prediction? The signs said Miranda would inherit Nicola's nature, including her musical ability and personality, possibly even "having her qualities of being kind, friendly, intelligent, and hard-working." This, in my view, is actually the most impressive part of the prediction. Although in some ways it's too early to tell—Miranda is only three years old—overall it's abundantly clear she is her mother's daughter, down to minute details. I know my genes are in there somewhere. I just don't know where. Miranda's strengths, weaknesses, and overall disposition appear to be her mother's.

We are not sure yet about Miranda's musical ability, since she is too young to play an instrument. All we can say for now is that she does have a tremendous sense of connection with music, along with strong preferences and an amazing memory for songs she has heard.

In terms of Nicola's personality, Miranda seems to have inherited that to an astonishing degree. Nicola's mother Pauline often remarks on how Nicola as a child was just like Miranda is now. The signs spoke of Miranda possibly being "kind" and "friendly." That prediction has proven strikingly accurate, as she is exceptionally sweet-natured. You might expect her father to say that, but nearly everyone who meets her remarks on it. It is easily her most outstanding quality.

She also seems to have fulfilled the predictions of being "intelligent and hard-working." We know a few child development experts and they all agree on her intelligence. One exclaimed, "Her cognitive skills are amazing. She is so smart!" As for the "hard-working" part, although she doesn't exactly have "work" to do right now, she has an unusual persistence with the tasks she does work at. For instance, she can sit by herself for long periods and put together a puzzle until it is complete.

As you can see, even though we don't have the complete picture yet, the signs appear to be on their way to one-hundred percent accuracy with Miranda. Nicola and I are frankly amazed. We remark on it regularly, as this is a time when Miranda's abilities and personality are coming out. And we wonder, how on earth did the signs know, years before she was even an embryo?

A miss and an unimpressive hit

I would be remiss if I gave the impression the signs' predictions were always stunningly accurate. I have experienced one unambiguous miss. I had two CMPEs that appeared to predict a specific event in the schooling of one of my children, five years away (I prefer to not share the details out of respect for those involved). The deadline came and went, and the event did not happen.

I had two thoughts about this. First, even though the specific event didn't occur, its overall context did move into place. That overall context consisted of predicted relationships between my child and two very different authority figures. These figures and the relationships with them actually did appear, very much as described in the signs, even though the predicted event did not.

Second, there is the common belief that the future is malleable, that it changes according to our choices. If true, this idea may provide a framework for understanding this failed prediction. I say that because, after initially predicting this event, the signs fell completely silent about it for five years, which is very uncharacteristic of them. In light of this, it seems *possible* to me that, in the meantime, different choices were made and that, as a result, the probable future changed.

I had another prediction that was a hit, but left me unimpressed. Over the course of three months, I had four signs that said a particular person would attack me over a certain issue, attempting to undermine me in the eyes of others (again, I prefer to not share the details). Before it could actually happen, I analyzed all four signs and wrote out a description of this predicted attack, complete with twenty-one characteristics.

About two weeks later, I was attacked by this person over this very issue in an attempt to undermine me in the eyes of others—just as the signs had said. A sign even accompanied this event, as if to mark the fulfilled prediction. I then reviewed those twenty-one predicted characteristics. By my reckoning, eleven had come true, five had partly come true, three had not come true, and two could only be ascertained in time. It was far from a perfect score, but the broad strokes of the prediction had indeed come to pass.

What did not come to pass, however, was the *magnitude* of the event as portrayed by the signs. In hindsight, I felt they had exaggerated. To be fair, there is a likelihood this same basic attack was repeated without my knowledge, and I have since been informed of one such case. Yet even if that is true, I think the signs were exaggerating.

Exaggeration, however, appears to be part of their nature. As I have said before, they delight in caricature. Therefore, if you have a predictive sign, bear in mind that the symbols used may be more extreme than the actual event of which they speak.

Y2K

I now want to tell the story of a predictive sign that went down in my mind as a spectacular failure, yet which eventually turned out to be an odd kind of spectacular success.

In 1998, I attended a meeting with some friends about the Y2K computer bug, which, of course, was expected by many to cause system-crippling computer crashes when clocks rolled over to January 1, 2000. My friends and I were gathering to discuss what safety measures, if any, we should take.

Two people arrived quite late. Upon arrival, they explained that on the way there they had independently come upon the same accident. A truck had lost control on a winding downhill road and rolled over three times. Both of them stopped to help. One of them called 911 and the other drove the truck's driver to his father's house.

After telling their story, they said they felt it must be a sign. Here we were meeting about a crash (the Y2K computer crash), specifically about what safety measures to take, and on the way to the meeting they had encountered a crash, and had responded with safety measures.

This didn't strike me as enough for a sign, but then one of them shared that earlier in the day he had watched the movie *Fearless*. It is about a man (played by Jeff Bridges) who is in a horrible plane crash. The plane rolls through a corn field, killing many onboard. When it finally stops, the man is utterly calm and unafraid, and leads passengers off the plane to safety. My friend thought it highly coincidental that shortly after watching a movie about a man leading people away from a plane crash, he found himself actually leading someone away from a vehicle crash.

That third event cinched it. In total, we had three crashes. In two of them, people I knew were together responding with safety measures. Two of the crashes were single-vehicle accidents in which the vehicle rolled a long distance. And in both of these crashes, a man led someone involved in the crash away from it. These and other parallels convinced me it was a CMPE.

I concluded that the two vehicle crashes were symbolic of Y2K. The vehicles, in other words, were really symbols for society as a whole "crashing" on that fateful date. The core of my interpretation, then, was this line: "Y2K will be like a societal plane crash."

Of course, that prediction turned out to be utterly wrong. If society was a plane, not only did that plane not crash on January 1, 2000, it didn't even encounter turbulence. In the aftermath of this, my trust in the signs took a real hit. Whenever the issue of their trustworthiness was mentioned, I would point out, "They *can* be wrong. They were wrong about Y2K."

Then came September 11, 2001. Shortly after the planes crashed into the World Trade Center, that sign from three years earlier began nagging at me. I couldn't help but notice the resemblance with 9/11. In both, the crash of an airplane represented so much more. It represented society-wide devastation. This resemblance prompted me (I think on the next day) to go back to my logs and look up that Y2K sign. When I finally pulled it up, I couldn't believe my eyes. The Y2K sign happened on September 11, 1998. It happened on *September 11*!

As you can imagine, I have been pondering this one for a long time. By no stretch can that sign be called accurate. It did not say "*9/11* will be like a societal plane crash." Yet it is also hard to call it a complete miss. It's difficult to avoid the impression that the signs knew more than they were saying. Think about it: On the crucial date of September 11, they were talking about a "societal plane crash," a plane crash that represented society-wide devastation. Perhaps I should have even focused more on that date, since part of the sign involved someone calling 911 *on* 9/11, a connection I didn't notice at the time. For all I know, that was the sign's attempt to refocus my attention away from the date of January 1 and onto September 11.

So what do we make of this? I cannot say for sure. However, I have noticed that this does fit a pattern I have observed. When the signs have some big theme in mind, they will often talk about it even in contexts that don't really relate. They are so focused on the big picture that they seem to lose no opportunity to speak of it. They are like a salesman who, when you say, "Nice day, isn't it?" responds with, "It would be an even better day if you owned this amazing new sports car."

An example of this is that "Shining Stranger" sign I recounted earlier. One of the events of that sign was our arbitration. Given the importance of that event for us, it would have been easy to assume the sign was about the arbitration, and was saying that it would free us up for good. Luckily, Greg read it accurately as being not about the arbitration (which didn't actually succeed in breaking our stalemate), but about the copyright itself. The arbitration was just an excuse for the signs to deliver their big message: "The Course will be freed!"

A sign about the preceding remarks

Remarkably, I just had a sign about the point I was making above! Halfway through writing the above paragraph, I paused to check my e-mail and received a message from an old friend of mine, Jannel Rap. She founded an organization called GINA for Missing Persons, which does wonderful work gaining attention for the missing. In her e-mail she told me that GINA had just sponsored over 200 events all around the world in the last ten weeks.

Jannel started the organization after a personal tragedy: On October 17, 2000, her sister Gina went missing and has never been seen again.

In her e-mail to me, Jannel said, "Check out our site when you get a chance... www.411Gina.org." So I did. I clicked on the link, and when the page loaded, a song titled "October 17," which Jannel wrote and sang, started to play. Here are its opening lyrics:

She said aren't you glad the rain is finally gone.
Then I heard the words for this song.
She didn't understand what she was sayin'.
But something deep inside of her must have heard me praying.

'Cause it's been raining since October 17.
I don't know if you know what I mean.
I've been treading water all this time.
At times it brings me comfort,
At times I lose my mind.

In a 2005 interview with the Orange County Register, Jannel explained that she wrote the song at the end of California's record-setting rainy season that year:

> The song wrote itself, she said, after a supermarket clerk recently remarked to her, "Aren't you glad the rain is finally gone?"
>
> It started raining last October 17, the fourth anniversary of her sister's disappearance.

I was immediately struck by the parallels between the song lyrics and my earlier line about the salesman ("[Signs] are like a salesman who, when you say, 'Nice day, isn't it?' responds with, 'It would be an even better day if you owned this amazing new sports car.'").

In these parallels, you have two people in conversation, an employee and a customer. One of them asks a trivial question about the good weather ("Nice day, isn't it?" "Aren't you glad the rain is finally gone?"). Normally, you expect a casual remark about the weather to elicit an equally casual remark in response. But in this case, it brings up for the other person a huge issue that is foremost on that person's mind. It becomes the opportunity for that person to express his or her big message about that issue, even though this message is only tangentially related to the original comment about the weather.

As you can see, these parallels sketch a very distinctive pattern. What are the odds I would write something that matches this distinctive pattern and then *minutes later* hear a song whose opening lines match this *same* distinctive pattern? It is clearly a CMPE.

And what it's saying is equally clear. It is backing up my point about how

CMPEs work. It is saying that, yes, they are like that salesman who will use any opportunity he can to get his big message across, even if it doesn't really fit the situation. Consequently, at times there is not a good fit between the big message the signs want to announce and the specific situations in which they announce it. As a prime example, the signs had something big to say about "societal plane crash" and September 11, but they spoke that message in the context of Y2K, making it appear that the message was *about* Y2K.

This latest CMPE strikes me as quite significant. This is a sign that is not so much about my life but about the signs themselves. The signs are telling us how they work. In the process, they are plausibly explaining that odd combination we have seen at times of accurate broad strokes and inaccurate details. I'll expand on this idea in the following chapter.

One last sign about 9/11

Since I'm on the topic of 9/11, I have one last predictive sign to share. On the evening of September 10, 2001, my son, Adam, who was twelve at the time, made an odd comment to me. He said that the definition of terrorism was no different than the definition of war. The only difference, he said, was that war was done by countries, not groups. I wanted to refute him, but found myself at a loss for words.

About eleven hours later, the first plane hit the World Trade Center. Like everyone else, we were glued to the TV in utter disbelief. All day long, news commentators were saying that what the terrorists did was an act of war. This equation of terrorism and war couldn't help but remind me of my son's comment the night before.

So I asked Adam why he had said that. His comment, it turns out, had been sparked by a computer game he was playing that evening called *Rainbow Six* (inspired by Tom Clancy's novel of the same name). In this game, it is 1999 and worldwide terrorism has sharply escalated, giving the anti-terrorist team (of which the player is part) plenty of juicy opportunities to ruthlessly respond to it. There is terrorism to fight in numerous high-profile targets, including the White House and Big Ben.

This was clearly a sign. The events of 9/11 had been foreshadowed in too many ways by Adam's game and comment the night before. Beyond the obvious parallels, though, I saw both a prediction and a warning.

The sign was treating Adam's comment as the moral of the story, and the point of his comment was *not* that terrorists are really waging war, but that a country going to war is no more justified than an act of terrorism. The sign, therefore, was implying that our country was going to war and that this war wouldn't be justified. Hence, just three days after September 11, when patriotic fervor was at its peak, I wrote the following interpretation: "Our country needs to watch how it responds, since a country going to war is not fundamentally different, or more justified, than an act of terrorism." I am now writing seven years later, in May 2008. Just last month, the Gallup Poll reported that 63% of Americans think the Iraq war was a mistake.

An economic collapse?

As we go to press, there is some material I need to add to the book. I was not planning to include it, as I didn't want this to be another book making huge predictions of scary times ahead. However, recent world events have made it logical to share what the signs have been saying.

For years the signs have been predicting an economic collapse that is analogous to the Great Depression. In early 2005 I pulled together a number of CMPEs on this topic, going back several years, and wrote this synthesis of what the signs had been saying:

> Economically, something big is coming. It will probably be akin to the Great Depression. It will end two decades of economic expansion in America, bursting a bubble that is at least partly based on collective self-deception. (February 2005)

The day after I finished this synthesis, Nicola had a sign confirming its main thrust. My interpretation of that new sign said, "Dark times are coming, times of economic depression" (February 25, 2005). Subsequent signs have continued to repeat this theme. They have spoken of "a looming fiscal crisis" (November 26, 2007) and "an economic collapse" (July 13 and August 14, 2007).

I am dearly hoping that the financial crisis currently under way isn't the beginning of this economic collapse. I frankly don't want to live through anything like the Great Depression. And at this point (late October 2008) we don't know how much the crisis in the financial sector will affect the real economy. But when everyone is talking about the worst financial crisis since the Great Depression, and when we even have the government warning of the exact same scenario as the signs ("Bush administration officials warned of a looming economic disaster akin to the Great Depression of the 1930s" if Congress didn't pass the bailout[16]), then I cannot escape the feeling that we might be on the brink of what the signs have been predicting.

Conclusion

You've seen the weakest and many of the strongest of my predictive signs. While their track record isn't perfect, I hope you have caught some of the same sense that I have. They don't just seem to be shooting in the dark. Rather, they seem, to a degree, to have their finger on the pulse of the future. They are often spectacularly accurate. And sometimes, even when they miss, you get the impression that they knew.

Chapter 9
The Depth of Their Insight

Just Kidding

I woke up one morning with a dream that a famous personality and I were an item. At least she thought we were, and I had somehow allowed her to think that. She was arriving at an *A Course in Miracles* conference, where I had just completed my presentation. I was trying to figure out how to tell her that I can't be with her. Before I could, she brought up how hurt she was about the e-mail she had just received from me. I had apparently begun this e-mail with a joke that I was going to have to dump her. Seeing her obvious hurt, I said, "I was only joking." She said that's not possible. "You can't say something like that without meaning it." I objected that if everything you say is taken as a direct reflection of your underlying intent, communication would fall apart. However, it did cross my mind that I had been trying to think of a way to end this relationship. Maybe she was right, I thought.

A couple of hours later I was teaching a morning Course class. The material we were covering that day (which I hadn't looked at before going into class) spoke of the need to recognize our thoughts for what they really are. So many of our thoughts, it said, are just attack thoughts in disguise. We dress up our anger and resentment in nice, well-intentioned forms, so we won't feel guilty. Then someone in the class chimed in, "We do that with humor. We use sarcasm to express our anger toward someone, and when they are offended, we say we were just kidding. But we weren't."

Of course, I immediately noticed the similarity with my dream. In both events, you express your negative sentiment in a statement that looks like a joke. Then, when the other person is hurt, you say you were just kidding, though in fact you really meant it. In both events, someone expresses this to me as a general observation about human communication, and does so at a *Course in Miracles* event at which I am teaching.

The CMPE was clearly about me. Not only had both events happened to me, but I had also been experiencing lingering guilt lately because my customary sarcastic humor had been especially barbed. Here, then, was my interpretation:

> I often use humor under the pretense that I really don't mean the unkind thing I've implied, when I really do. I need to recognize these comments for what they are, for they do cause others pain.

People close to me had given me this message for years. And I did hear them and try to rein in my sarcasm. However, it was one thing to have other people tell me this, and quite another to have a sign come to specifically deliver this message. As you might imagine, it made the message go in much further.

It went in still further when I realized I had received an extremely parallel sign on the exact same day a year before. This other sign also featured me teaching a Course class about the importance of looking at our attack thoughts. And similar to the new one, its message was that I need to look at my own attack thoughts, because regardless of what I tell myself, they really do have an effect on others.

In the previous chapter, we saw that CMPEs display an ability to see into the future. Yet they not only see far, they also see deeply. They have an uncanny ability to see into the depths of a situation or a person, quickly identifying the underlying dynamics at the heart of that situation or person. That depth of insight is what we will explore in this chapter.

To show you this quality at work, I will take you through a case study consisting of six CMPEs about a friend of mine whom I will call Steve. These signs show Steve navigating through a variety of psychological, relationship, and career issues, which turn out to be surprisingly related. They take us into the unhealed regions of Steve's psyche, at times perhaps to an uncomfortable degree. Yet Steve is no different than the rest of us. He is outwardly well-adjusted, yet inwardly carries the typical load of human wounds and complexes. CMPEs have a way of hitting these nails right on the head, no matter who we are. Yet they also are adept at pointing the way out, and they are quick to praise us when we head in that direction.

One side-benefit of this case study is that we get to see CMPEs other than my own. Five of the six CMPEs happened to Steve. The final one happened right in front of my eyes, yet I didn't notice it (Steve did). Only one CMPE—the third—happened to me. Yet all of them fit the four-point model perfectly. And the one that happened to me is indistinguishable in its message from those that happened to Steve. Here, then, you get to see CMPEs operating in someone's life other than mine and Nicola's, though what you find out is that they fit the exact same pattern.

1. Steve's Little Part

Steve received a coaching session from a woman named Kelly who was training to be a personal coach. The topic he wanted to work on was his lack of passion around the pastoral counseling program he was taking.

As the session began, Kelly quickly zeroed in on Steve's longstanding split between his spirituality and his humanity. His humanity wanted to connect with the world and with people. Yet his spirituality was largely about renouncing his humanity and retreating into a contemplative life, where his relationship with God was laced with fantasy and escapism. Since he saw pastoral counseling as linked with his spirituality, he associated it with the sacrifice of his human needs. Hence, his lack of passion for it.

During the session, Steve realized he had been carrying the dream that someday, after he completed his pastoral counseling degree, his spirituality and humanity would finally fuse into one. He would be out there serving people through pastoral counseling; serving them but also truly joining with them. Thus, his spirituality—expressed in the service—and his humanity—expressed in the joining—would come together in one and the same function.

The big light bulb that went on in this session was that there were people around him *now* that needed his help. They had been there all along, yet he had overlooked them while he dreamed of a distant future as a selfless helper. Suddenly, he felt guilty for all the opportunities to give and receive that he had lost. Yet the opportunities were still there, and he realized they were his chance to resolve the split in him between his spirituality and humanity.

Directly after his coaching session, Steve went to a *Course in Miracles* class I was teaching. The topic (which no one knew beforehand but me) was "Our Little Part." The main theme was that while we worry about larger problems beyond our sphere of influence, we tend to overlook "our little part," which consists of serving and joining with *particular people* who are in our lives now. This quote is from the handout I gave out at class:

> There are certain key things within [our sphere of influence], things we might easily overlook, things we might stand in front of for years without noticing, but things that have the power to change lives. That was certainly the case with Helen and Bill [Helen Schucman and Bill Thetford, the two people who "scribed" *A Course in Miracles*]. For years they didn't notice that right in front of them was this door marked "join with your brother," and that if they walked through this door, they would change their own lives and thousands of other lives forever.

It wasn't hard to see the parallels between these two events: While in a session with a coach or teacher, Steve had received a vital message. The message is that our true function consists of something very close at hand. It consists of serving and joining with people who are in our lives now. Particular people are right in front of us who need our help. Yet we may overlook for a long time the opportunities they hold out to us. We may avoid our function, our "little part," by focusing on something much grander and much further away.

It was not a dazzling set of parallels, but it was a definite sign. Steve asked me to interpret it for him, and a couple of months later I got around to writing this interpretation:

> Rather than waiting until some glorious day when he has a pastoral counseling practice and is living a great life of healing oth-

ers, Steve needs to serve and connect and join with those in his life now. The opportunities are all around him, if he will only take them. This will pull him out of his fantasy mode, will help him feel alive again about the spiritual path, and help him heal his split between his spirituality and his humanity.

As I was finishing this interpretation, I was surprised to receive a call from Steve. He wanted to tell me about what he felt was another sign.

2. Strange Days

A few days before he called me, Steve had seen his therapist. Together they discussed Steve's need to move on from a recently ended relationship with Jennifer. He wanted to go forward with his life and find a fulfilling relationship that could lead to marriage. Yet he still felt deeply attached to Jennifer. She had told him she would be dating another man, yet in his mind he was still in an intimate relationship with her. At this point, Steve confessed to his therapist that he lived a great deal of his life in fantasy.

The therapist said that when he felt attracted to a woman, he should act on the opportunity and see if there was real potential there. In other words, he should get out of his fantasy life and start taking initiative to create a real relationship in the real world. Steve left the session feeling empowered and ready to move forward.

Not long afterward, he went home and ate dinner in front of the TV, watching a movie called *Strange Days*. The lead character, Lenny, is a former LAPD cop, who now lives a hollow existence selling "SQUID" recordings. SQUID is a futuristic technology that records people's experiences directly from their cerebral cortex. This allows any user to see, hear, and feel exactly what the original person did. Lenny's most prized possessions are the SQUID recordings he made of cherished moments with his former girlfriend, Faith. Even though she heartlessly rejected him, we see him playing these recordings, living more inside them than in his actual life.

Meanwhile, his friend Mace is a woman who has stood faithfully by him and secretly loves him, despite being disgusted by his addictive attachment to a bygone romance. His life is lived between these two women. One is the memory of someone who dumped him when he was no longer convenient. The other is a living, breathing woman who continues to stand by him, despite her pain at seeing him living the wrong life. In the end, he has to make a choice between these two—the choice between fantasy and reality.

As he watched the movie, the feeling grew in Steve that he was watching an eerie caricature of himself, caught between living in his memories of Jennifer and moving forward into a real relationship in the present. It was definitely a sign (the parallels are even more detailed than this brief description suggests). Here is the interpretation I wrote for him:

> Steve is still obsessed with Jennifer, still fantasizing about her, even though they are no longer together….He is living in the past. He must choose to move on. He needs to let the fantasy of her go and be present to his actual life and to the opportunities in that life for a new, healthier relationship. He needs to move on from Jennifer and begin trying to cultivate a relationship with a woman who can be a real partner, a woman who pulls him into reality, not out of it.

3. "Steve's Little Part" and "Strange Days"

Recall that Steve phoned me about the "Strange Days" sign *while* I was writing up the "Little Part" sign, even though ten weeks had passed since that first one. This conjunction of events made for a brand new CMPE, simply because the new sign shared so many parallels with the old one.

In both cases, there is a sign about Steve that he has asked me to process for him. Event 1 consists of Steve having a session with a coach or therapist in which he discusses an emotional pattern he wants to be free of. The conclusion is that, to be free of this emotional pattern, Steve needs to get out of his fantasy bubble, in which he spends his time dreaming of what he used to have ("Strange Days") or one day could have ("Steve's Little Part"). To get out of this bubble, Steve needs to be present to his current life and focus on joining with people in the present. The session is then followed by event 2 (a class or movie), which strikingly mirrors the contents of the session, thus making for a sign.

What are the odds of me processing one CMPE that has all these characteristics, and right as I am doing that, hearing from Steve about *another* CMPE with these same characteristics?

As an aside, I should mention that this is a common occurrence. Signs gravitate to other signs, so that working on a previous sign will often become event 1 of a new sign. This really is a sixth kind of interconnectedness between signs, to add to the five I described in the last chapter.

4. The Monk and the Wild Woman

A few months later, Steve was having another session with his therapist. He was discussing his (still over) relationship with Jennifer and how sexuality was a key part of the split between his spirituality and his humanity. His therapist pointed out that Steve has a pattern of swinging back and forth between the two sides. He finds his sexuality so problematic that he retreats like a monk into an almost cloistered contemplative life, but then feels inevitably dragged back toward his sexuality. Yet giving into its pull causes such guilt that he retreats back to being a monk, and the cycle starts over. Neither side seems to be a healthy expression; both are filled with fantasy.

His therapist, in fact, offered his opinion that Steve is attracted to "taboo-type relationships," relationships that can never really come to fruition. This explained the attraction to Jennifer, who turned out to be mentally unstable, as well as to previous women who were completely unavailable to Steve.

That evening, Steve went home planning to focus on his homework for his pastoral counseling program, but decided to turn the TV on instead. He happened upon a scene from the movie *The Name of the Rose*. In this scene, a young monk is in a foreign monastery at night and discovers he is not alone. Out from the shadows comes a dirty and disheveled young peasant woman. She is beautiful and sensual, but clearly not in full possession of her faculties. While watching this scene, Steve can't help but be reminded of his former girlfriend Jennifer. Without a word spoken (she doesn't seem able to speak), the peasant girl initiates what becomes the monk's first sexual encounter.

For the rest of the movie, the monk is torn between his monastic vows and a totally unworkable sexual relationship—an exact mirror of what Steve had just discussed with his therapist. He finally chooses to remain a monk, after which he never sees the girl again. As the movie ends, he tells us that he never regretted his decision, "for I learned from my master much that was wise and good and true." But then he says,

> And yet, now that I'm an old, old man, I must confess that of all the faces that appear to me out of the past, the one I see most clearly is that of the girl, of whom I have never ceased to dream these many long years. She was the only earthly love of my life. Yet I never knew, nor ever learned, her name.

As the viewer, we are unsure how to take this. Is it touching or pathetic? Its meaning within the sign, however, is clear. It symbolically depicts Steve maintaining his split: outwardly choosing his monk-like existence, devoting his life to what is "wise and good and true," yet all the while inwardly fantasizing of a brief relationship with a young woman who lacked the capacity for real relationship. This is clearly not a positive symbol. It tells of a sad future for Steve if he does not heal the split within him.

5. Vanilla Sky

In the previous sign, we saw the therapist's insight that Steve was attracted to relationships that could never come to fruition. That sign then backed this up with the vivid image of a highly educated monk falling for a developmentally disabled peasant girl—an unfeasible union if there ever was one!

Interestingly, the signs had brought me to a similar insight several months earlier. I had been processing the first three CMPEs in this collection, and they had jogged my memory of an earlier CMPE I had forgotten. Three years before, Steve had a sign that was so parallel that it makes your jaw drop. The form of it was eerily familiar: a talk with a helper followed by a strikingly parallel movie (*Vanilla Sky*). In this movie (just as in *Strange Days*) a man lives in a high-tech fantasy of being with a woman who has long since rejected him. Instead, he must choose to awaken to present-day reality. The message of the sign was also eerily familiar. Here is how I had interpreted it three years earlier:

> Steve wants the love of some group—[blank]—and some person—[blank]—more than anything, a love that seems impossible to really obtain. As a result, his life has been in a holding pattern for a long time. He has opted for going off into a fantasy life which includes a fantasy of getting this love. Instead, he needs to open his eyes and wake up to reality. He needs to face real life, with all its paradox. He needs to live a life that comes from something real within him.

Here, of course, was the exact same pattern of Steve getting lost in the fantasy of a love that can never be. But here was also something new: two additional examples of this pattern (the two blanks). With now three examples spanning at least three years, I realized that Steve's attachment to fantasy went deeper than I thought. I realized he is not attracted to certain relationships *in spite of* their impossibility. He is attracted to them *because of* their impossibility. Ironically, he wanted a fantasy that could *never come true*. Here is what I wrote him in attempting to capture what the signs were saying:

> It's almost like something in you wants to stay in fantasy…like you don't want the fantasy to come true, because then you'd be in reality, not in fantasy. It's like there's something inherently scary to you about being in reality.

I found this insight surprising and counterintuitive—who would guess that someone actually doesn't *want* his dreams to come true? Yet I also thought it was accurate. After all, Steve's therapist ended up seeing more or less the same thing. Clearly, in trying to carry out the signs' counsel and join with people in his current life, Steve was swimming against a deep undertow.

6. Celebration of Steve

A year after the somewhat dark string of CMPEs I've been relating, another one came along that struck a whole different note. In this CMPE, a friend and longtime helper of Steve's (the helper from "Vanilla Sky") felt he had turned a hugely significant corner in his journey. She had for years been trying to help him move into his function of serving others, and she was convinced he was at last genuinely doing that.

Indeed, the evidence of this was there for anyone to see. For example, Steve would take my older children to dinner or a basketball game in Phoenix. Sometimes I would run into him coming out of the health food store after he took a local homeless man on a free shopping trip. It was obvious that service had become a cornerstone of his life.

This turning point was so important for Steve's friend and coach, not to mention for him, that she wanted to celebrate it. She took the unusual step of bringing a cake to a study group Steve attends. There, in a departure from the group's normal agenda, she did a kind of tribute to him. She read the group a letter she had written for his ordination in pastoral counseling. It detailed the ways he regularly demonstrated his dedication to God and service to others. The letter amazed everyone. There were so many things on the list, yet they were all true. The group realized that, with no fanfare and little recognition, Steve had been quietly living out his convictions on multiple fronts. It felt truly appropriate that this was finally being celebrated.

At the same meeting, another woman broke with the usual format and read a kind of tribute to another man who had stood up for his convictions and performed an important service. This man's accomplishments went unrecognized for a long time, until others made them known and they were finally honored. He had been important to her for years, and his recent transition meant enough to her that she decided to bring news of it to the group. All of this, of course, was equally true of the celebration of Steve. This list of parallels was long enough to qualify the events as a CMPE.

The second man was Hugh Thompson. He was the helicopter pilot who, in 1968, landed his helicopter in the middle of the My Lai massacre in Vietnam to rescue civilians and prevent further violence on the part of his comrades. Thompson acted purely on principle. He never sought recognition for his deeds, and indeed, when he returned home, it seemed to him that he, rather than those who carried out the massacre, was viewed as the guilty party. Finally, in the late-80's, a professor launched a letter-writing campaign that led to Thompson being awarded the Soldier's Medal in 1998—thirty years after My Lai. He had recently died, and the woman was reading to the group a newspaper article marking his death.

This CMPE was a welcome change from the earlier ones. Having likened Steve to some pretty messed up characters, the signs were now likening him to a war hero who took decisive action based on pure principle. Steve was doing what the signs had asked—serving and connecting with the people in his current life—and they were responding by (quite literally) celebrating his progress.

The quality of these messages

These six CMPEs, spanning four years, form a very tight cluster. On the level of form, in four CMPEs, event 1 is a session with a helper in which Steve receives crucial insights about key psychological patterns of his. Then in three signs, this is followed by a movie whose protagonist is caught in those same patterns; specifically, caught up in a dream life about a love that can never be. As if to underscore this interrelatedness, two of the signs ("Steve's Little Part" and "Strange Days") bumped into each other to create a new sign.

What we are most interested in here, however, is the quality of their insight. So let's look at that issue.

On the level of content, the messages are the opposite of a chaotic hodgepodge. Instead, they are extremely consistent, so much so that together they add up to a single larger vision.

This vision covers an impressive variety of specific issues: getting over Jennifer, moving on to a healthier relationship, bringing passion into his pastoral counseling studies, moving into his true function, healing the split between his spirituality and his humanity, and healing his issues around sexuality.

The signs then wade into this almost bewildering variety and boil it down to a surprisingly simple picture. The answer to each of Steve's problems, they say, lies in him traveling the single road from *fantasy* to *reality*. In case after case, we saw them bring things back to this very basic issue.

The fantasy side is given specific shape. The signs depict Steve fantasizing about being a great helper, or about an escapist relationship with God, but mainly about his failed romance with Jennifer.

The reality side is also given specific, and quite practical, shape. Coming into reality is not some vague concept. Rather, it equals Steve coming into his present life and connecting with the people who are there. This especially takes the form of serving people in his current life, but it also means acting on promising relationships with women he meets.

In speaking of this journey from fantasy to reality, the signs display what I consider a remarkable depth of insight. They suggest that Steve *in principle* wants to stay in fantasy and out of reality. As a result, he is attracted to fantasies that can *never* become reality.

In all this, the signs show an ability to see beneath the surface. If you knew Steve socially, you would probably never suspect any of these things about him. He comes off as an outgoing, affable, sincere, endearing person, always willing to help out. He certainly does not look like he's lost in fantasy.

However, if you know him really well, you realize the signs have nailed him. Indeed, these signs incorporate and expand on the insights of two of Steve's long-time helpers (who show up in two signs each), one of them a licensed clinical psychologist. Finally, their message rings true to Steve himself. These CMPEs, in other words, appear to have that most important characteristic: accuracy.

The CMPEs have presented a vision whose quality is so high that I expect we would feel fortunate to receive its equal from any therapist. This vision weaves together a variety of personal issues into an extremely simple picture, one that has both depth and practicality, and that above all seems accurate to those who would know.

This is hardly the sort of vision we would expect to come out of a series of random conjunctions of events. Yet somehow it did—at least the conjunctions *seemed* random. Let's forget for a moment, though, where it came from. Let's just ask ourselves: If a vision like this came to us from *any* source, wouldn't it garner our immediate respect?

How CMPEs deal with situations

The way we have seen the signs deal with Steve is a great example of how they deal with situations in general. Indeed, what we see here is an expanded version of the same pattern we saw in the previous chapter with the signs about my writing. We can see that pattern as having three parts.

First, the signs *focus* on what they see as the key elements of the situation. They wade into a complex situation, bypass the noise, and immediately zero in on what they regard as the central issue. They will then return to this same issue, each time from a slightly different angle, each time adding new facets to an ever-enlarging vision. As you begin to grasp this vision, you will usually be able to look back and realize that, amazingly, its essence was all there in the very first sign.

Second, they identify the core *problem*. They quickly locate the hidden anchor that lies buried at the heart of the situation and keeps it from moving. They then hold it up to the light with unflinching honesty. Rather than sugarcoat the problem, they usually do just the opposite—they caricature it (remember "Krusty the Father" from Chapter 3?). This can smart if you're on the receiving end—since the problem is often inside you—but it does serve to bring the problem forcefully and vividly into your awareness. Warning: If you want your mistakes and character defects conveniently rationalized and excused, do not work with CMPEs!

Third, they point out the *solution* and reinforce any movement in its direction. However negative CMPEs may get, their ultimate intent seems clearly positive. They want to move us forward, out of the problem. They therefore constantly point us in the direction of the way out. They often frame this way out in specific and practical ways (though they rarely provide the kind of detailed blueprints we would prefer). And when we move in their direction, even a little bit, they are quick to reinforce that. They are just as quick to praise as they are to criticize, and their praise can be lavish.

In all of this, their counsel is tailor-made to fit this particular situation.

They never dish out one-size-fits-all advice. Rather, their message is always specially crafted to fit the unique contours and essence of the situation at hand. This tight fit means their counsel appears to be accurate, especially to those in a position to know.

The three parts I have outlined clearly constitute a *change-oriented* pattern. CMPEs do not coddle you and tell you everything is wonderful, that all your choices are "right for you," and all your character traits are an essential part of your unique beauty. They don't want to lull you into a denial-based complacency that grants the illusion of peace in the midst of a chronic problem. They give you the hard truth because they aim for change.

Does their advice work when followed?

As I just pointed out, CMPEs are trying to move us toward the solution. This raises an inevitable question: Does their advice work out? When followed, does it actually solve things? This is an extremely subjective issue, since there is always the question of how well we followed their advice. However, having acknowledged this subjectivity, I will offer my observations.

My experience is that, yes, when followed, their advice seems to work out—*if* we understand that the actual advice may be the specific solution offered or it may just be the general direction indicated. We saw in the previous chapter that CMPEs are singleminded about getting across their big message, and will do so even in specific contexts that don't quite apply. This grates against our assumption that the specifics are what is important. The signs, however, seem to see it the other way around: the big message is what is important; the specifics are just examples or illustrations of that big message. In our eyes, what is important is the figure; in their eyes, it is the ground.

It is crucial that we are aware of this difference in perspective. On an action level, what it means is this: When a CMPE tells us to do something specific, that specific thing *may* immediately get the hoped-for result, and it may just be there to point us in the right general direction.

We have seen examples of both in this book. For example, with "The

Treasure House" (Chapter 5), the CMPEs about the right house for us paid off in a big way. Without them, we quite simply wouldn't be in this house. With "Family Comes First" (Chapter 4), our plan for the new year that prioritized family time worked out beautifully. With the sign about the conclusion to my book *Return to the Heart of God* (Chapter 7), reader feedback on that conclusion has been unusually enthuasiastic, especially about how personal it was—the very thing the sign emphasized.

In contrast, "The Bucket Brigade" (Chapter 1) was an example of a specific solution that didn't solve everything but did point us in the right direction. We did publish the introductory book recommended by that CMPE (*Path of Light*), and we did form an energetic bucket brigade to get it printed and publicized. Yet the book didn't become the spectacular success that swept us out of our financial difficulties. On the other hand, it did become the best-selling book we had ever published (and we've published a great many), and it did resurrect our publishing program, which was a key factor in the Circle doubling its income over the next three years.

After the book was out, the CMPEs continued to call us in the same general direction. They continued to push us to form a more efficient, bucket brigade-like team, and they continued to urge us to publish, promising that one day our publishing *would* reach a much larger audience. This is typical for the signs. Even when a specific course of action doesn't deliver what we hope for, the signs don't miss a beat. They keep right on urging us forward in the same general direction, as if nothing has changed. Noticing this, in fact, is what tipped me off to the idea that signs care more about the big message than the specifics.

At any rate, when a CMPE recommends a specific course of action, it behooves you to consciously remind yourself that this action may have the desired result and that it may simply represent the right overall direction, or perhaps something in between. Try to keep an open mind about this issue, even while you take steps to implement the specific action.

Personal evaluations of their trustworthiness

I am deeply impressed with the quality of the counsel offered by the signs. This really goes beyond specific pieces of advice that have proven fruitful. There is just something about their voice. There is a ring of truth in it. They aren't wishy-washy—they adopt a viewpoint, but it is a viewpoint that doesn't seem to succumb to the biases, short-sightedness, and inconsistencies that hobble our viewpoints. Signs really do appear to be surveying things from above, taking in the whole picture, seeing far down the road, yet also seeing deeply into the current situation and each person involved. It is this indefinable quality, this ring of truth, that keeps me following them.

Yet, of course, that is just my own personal sense. To give you a perspective from slightly outside of mine, I have asked Nicola and Greg to share their opinions of the signs' counsel. Granted, their opinions are very much like my own, but they are also the only two other people I know of who have worked seriously and at length with this phenomenon. To make their observations as independent as possible, I asked them to put those observations on paper before they read this chapter. Here are the questions I asked them to answer:

> How much trust do you have in the signs? And to the extent that you do trust them, why do you, given that they have at times asked you to do things you didn't want to do, been critical of you, and made promises that have not yet come true?

I will let them conclude the chapter.

Greg

I have been working with signs for several years now, and have come to trust them more than any other form of guidance. Why? First, they are the most objective form of guidance I've ever encountered. Of course, since they need to be interpreted, *some* subjectivity will inevitably enter in. But the events that constitute signs are not manufactured by my own mind, so if I follow the rules for identifying and interpreting signs carefully, I can get a message so clear that another interpreter following the same rules would get the same thing (as I've seen when Robert and I compared interpretations of the same sign). I find this truly uncanny. In my mind, this greatly increases the likelihood that what I get is truly coming from a source independent of my own wishful thinking.

Second, signs have given me sound advice that has worked out when I've followed it. They have given me effective resolutions to problems in my life, resolutions that were often unexpected and proved to be the most loving course of action for all concerned. At times, they have given me predictions about events that have turned out to be true. Even when I've resisted their counsel initially, I've found that following it was far more beneficial than anything I would have done on my own.

Third, as my signs have accumulated over time, they have painted a "big picture" of my life that is amazingly consistent and integrated. In particular, they have provided a detailed picture of my "calling"—what I'm here on earth to do. This has given me a deep sense of conviction about my life's purpose and meaning, something I think everyone yearns for. While there are still plenty of unanswered questions, I feel very clear about the direction I'm going and feel confident that more will be revealed as I go along.

Nicola

I have a huge amount of trust in the signs. There are a number of reasons why I trust them, even though they have been critical of me or have made promises that have not yet come true. One is simply that they have made a good many promises that *have* come true, promises that have been detailed and specific and absolutely unknowable in advance (such as the sex and nature of our future daughter, including the fact that I *would* have a baby when I had all but given up hope). There have been enough signs over the years, with enough specific information that has come true, to give me hope and trust in the signs that haven't yet come true. Conversely, the signs that have made predictions or promises that have simply not come true to any degree are absolutely negligible. I can't actually think of any as I write this.

In terms of the overall quality of their message, I find that I think of the signs as a wise, impartial advisor. They don't play favorites (though they're not afraid of taking sides in any given situation). Even when their perspectives are critical of me or ask me to take some difficult action, there is always a context that makes total sense—a context in which it is easy to see that a broader picture than simply my comfort zone is being considered. If someone is consistently giving advice from a perspective that is higher than yours—that takes all parties into account equally, doesn't play favorites, and genuinely has an eye on the bigger picture—why would you not trust that? Isn't that what we all want when we claim to want spiritual guidance? Some higher perspective on our affairs, which also includes a higher perspective on others' affairs, that can see how our actions affect the whole, and encourages us in a direction that has a positive impact on all concerned?

Chapter 10
The Philosophy of the Signs

Laura's Special Function

Several years ago Laura discovered she had a gift. Whenever someone asked her for her advice on some personal issue, the words would just flow out of her. She felt as if she were literally being "spoken through." Even though afterward she would second-guess herself and wonder what on earth she just said, people consistently came back and said that her advice was exactly what they needed to hear. Many told her she had changed their lives. What was her reaction to this surprising gift? "Of course I decided I should stop talking to people. I was that freaked out. I felt no control over these conversations. I convinced myself this couldn't be good."

This all changed, however, when she committed to taking a year-long *A Course in Miracles* study program (the one that kept me so busy in the "Family Comes First" sign from Chapter 4). The program frequently stressed the theme from the Course that giving leads to receiving rather than depletion. She therefore tried to find a particular way in which she could give. Then she remembered those conversations she used to have. She said, "I really missed these conversations! I would feel so connected and flowing and I would say to friends that I felt that it fed my soul and I knew that it was my purpose."

As a result, she chose to volunteer on the phones at a local crisis center. That way, she could use her gift, but do so anonymously. She immediately began experiencing the same thing she had before—feeling completely guided in her words and getting reinforcing feedback in return.

Yet there was one way this giving really did feel like depletion: "I have been recently struggling with this one caller, Peter, who is trapped by his childhood abuse....I know other volunteers have been feeling challenged by him as well because he can yell at them and sometimes hang up. I don't always get the same people, but I have been getting him almost every time."

This reached the point where, one day when she was scheduled to go into the crisis center, she was questioning going in. She just didn't know if she could face the prospect of talking to Peter that day. Indeed, she was questioning whether she would go back at all.

In the midst of this questioning, she sat down and read that day's material in her *A Course in Miracles* study program. It was a section from the Course along with commentary by my colleague Greg Mackie. This section teaches that God's way, which consists of pure love and giving, may seem like madness, since we fear that a life of unconditional giving will drain us dry. But it is actually sane, for giving is how we receive.

We learn this through what this section calls our *special function*— similar to what is often called our life purpose. Our special function is a specific role through which we give to others. It is a concrete way in which we can learn that generosity actually fills us up, rather than drains us dry. This role takes a different shape for each of us, being designed around our particular strengths, our unique gifts. It has to be tailor-made for us, so we can embrace it as our own. This will allow us to learn through it a lesson we deeply resist, the lesson that giving as God gives is *sanity*, not suicide.

As Laura was reading these various ideas, she encountered this paragraph from Greg:

> Our special function is our own unique form of [expressing God's way]. It is forgiving Joe for that unkind remark; extending healing to Sue, who has come to us for help; working a miracle for Peter, who feels trapped by his abused childhood. How better can we learn the sanity of love than by seeing its transforming effects in our own lives and in the lives of everyone we encounter?

As you can imagine, when she read that line "working a miracle for Peter, who feels trapped by his abused childhood," her eyes practically sprang out of their sockets! The very question she was wrestling with looked as if it were being specifically answered there on the page. She described her reaction to me in an e-mail later that day:

> It completely spoke to me and I could not believe what I was reading. I had to read it again and ***I knew it*** was meant for me specifically!! I could not believe the name was right—sometimes we don't know their real names. Then I decided I was definitely going in tonight and everything was going to be OK—I didn't have to figure it out. I am typing fast because I am on my way to the center right now!!

The material she read was an uncanny mirror of Laura's situation. What stands out, of course, is the incredible parallel about helping "Peter, who feels trapped by his abused childhood." Yet the parallels continued. In both events, helping Peter was just a concrete expression of the special function (which Laura had called her "purpose"), a special form of giving that is particularly suited to the individual. And that special function, in turn, was a concrete expression of the Course's principle that giving is receiving. This entire three-level structure was present in both events, where it was also pervaded by resistance, by the fear that this giving will mean being depleted rather than filled up.

Laura's resistance, of course, was on the verge of getting the better of her. She was questioning helping Peter, which to a certain degree meant questioning the entire structure I just outlined. This CMPE, however, specifically answered her question about going in that day, and in the process answered so much more. It affirmed she should keep volunteering at the crisis center. And it affirmed that her gift for inspired advice really is her special function, the particular way she will learn that giving is receiving. She, of course, had already sensed this, saying, "I felt that it fed my soul and I knew that it was my purpose." So the sign was really just backing up a prior feeling of hers, but it was clearly a feeling that needed backing up!

After this sign, Laura's hesitancy to man the crisis hotline vanished. Since then, she says, "My experiences have been amazing and life-changing for me as well as the callers.... The feedback I receive from the callers still blows me away; I don't know if I will ever get used to it." In the intervening two years, she has gotten more involved at the center. She has been asked to become a trainer, she personally reorganized and bought furniture for the call room, and she is assisting with the center's fundraising. She concludes, "I have no doubts that I am supposed to be here and what I am supposed to be doing."

Do CMPEs have a particular philosophy? I don't mean the word "philosophy" in an academic sense. We won't be examining how signs weigh in on epistemology or metaphysics. Instead, I mean the word in the more popular sense of a "philosophy of life"—a system of values by which one lives.

Of course, from a skeptical standpoint, we have no reason to suspect that CMPEs would have any philosophy at all. In such a view, they are just random conjunctions of events. How could a coherent philosophy emerge from a pile of random occurrences?

Yet in fact, it doesn't take long to see certain values running through sign after sign. You may have noticed this yourself. For instance, we have seen a number of CMPEs that were critical of some form of withdrawal from others, whether that was me not spending enough time with my family or Steve withdrawing from others into his fantasy life.

We have also seen CMPEs that merely offer concrete advice not particularly suggestive of larger values. (e.g., "Your signs book should definitely include a how-to component.") Yet even in cases like these, when you add in different signs on that same subject, you realize this concrete advice is really a distillation of a larger, value-laden message. (e.g., "When you perceive a gap between you and your audience, rather than backing away, bridge that gap.")

In most CMPEs, the values are implicit; they're in the background. In this chapter, however, we will look at signs where the values are in the foreground. This will enable us to get a sense of their philosophy. And this, in turn, will help us evaluate the signs themselves. What does their philosophy tell us about their character? Does their philosophy call upon the better angels of our nature? Does it support the idea that CMPEs come from a higher place? Hopefully, this chapter will help us answer these questions.

Service with a Smile

On August 27, 1999, I was set to lead the meeting of a spiritual group I had been part of for a long time. I was going to focus on a story in which a man responds to an outrageous request with an extraordinary act of generosity. To apply the message of this story, I was going to ask each of us in the group to recall a recent request from another member of the group. Then I would ask us all to make an inner commitment to answer that request like the man in the story did.

As the meeting began, I was about to launch into my talk when another member, Alexandra, suddenly spoke up. Before the meeting, she had been speaking with Susan, my wife at the time. About three weeks earlier, Susan and I had moved to a new house, moving not only our personal belongings, but also the Circle of Atonement's offices and storage. Susan had been sharing with Alexandra how overwhelmed she felt, as unpacked boxes were still scattered all over the house. Alexandra, who had already gone above and beyond the call of duty in helping us move, nonetheless found herself filled with concern for Susan.

So she proposed that we turn that night's meeting into a "let's help the Perrys unpack" meeting. Some members were agreeable, but some were understandably resistant. The fact was that the Perrys had already received an enormous amount of help. Further, we had accumulated a huge amount of stuff ("stuff" being a charitable description) and some felt that our unpacking nightmare was thus a pit we had dug for ourselves. Moreover, people were curious about the meeting I had planned and wanted me to carry on with that.

After some delicate discussion, we decided to do both: to have a brief version of the meeting I had planned followed by everyone helping Susan and me get situated in our new place. So I commenced with reading the story I had brought.

The story was called "Service with a Smile."[17] In it, a man shares a childhood event that became a lifelong lesson. An old woman shows up at his father's furniture store and says, "I bought a sofa from your store and the leg fell off. I want to know when you're going to fix it." The son assumes they won't be fixing her old sofa (she says she bought it ten years earlier) for free. But his father replies that they will go that afternoon.

On the way back, the father asks what is bothering the son. "You know that I want to go to college," he says. "If we drive around fixing old sofas for free, we'll go broke." The father then reveals what was really going on:

> "You had to learn how to do that repair job anyway. Besides, you missed the most important part. You didn't notice the store tag when we flipped the couch over. She bought it from Sears."
> "You mean we did that job for nothing and she's not even our customer?"
> Dad looked me in the eye and said, "She is now."

Two days later, the woman came in and bought several thousand dollars' worth of furniture from the son. He concludes by saying,

> I've been selling for 30 years since that day. I have had the highest closing average in every organization I have represented because I treat customers with respect.

We had an invigorating discussion sparked by this uplifting story. However, when I came to my concluding exercise, I got distinctly uncomfortable. As I said, my plan was to have us all think of a recent request from another member of the group, and then respond like the father had in the story. Well, we had all just *had* a request from a member of the group— a request to help the Perrys! Given this, my exercise now had the effect of pressuring everyone into helping *my* family. I wasn't the only one who was squirming in my seat at this point.

It was not until the night was over (and our house was in much better shape, thanks to everyone's help) that I noticed just how coincidental the evening had been. The story I shared was uncannily similar to the story that had played out in our meeting in response to Alexandra's suggestion. Both contained the same basic cast of characters who somehow managed to follow the same basic plotline.

Both stories feature the woman of the house, who needs help with her old furnishings, even though by normal standards she probably does not deserve it. Her need reaches the ears of the hero of the story (the father, Alexandra), who instantly sets aside concerns about what is fair and reasonable, and decides to help out anyway. Then there is a third party (the son, the group members), who is induced to help, but grumbles about it, saying that it's not deserved. Finally, both stories were really about prompting members of our group to generously respond to a request for help from another member.

It is hard to imagine that two such similar stories would coincide purely by chance. It was obviously a CMPE. And just as obviously, its message was calling us to set aside considerations of merit and help someone in spite of our feeling that this person didn't deserve it.

Normally, of course, our helpfulness is carefully gauged to match other people's perceived deservedness. Every step we go beyond what we think they deserve feels like wading through mud. Finally, we simply stop, even if they are still in need. What this CMPE is calling us to do is to remove this constraint from our helpfulness, to stop limiting our kindness by our estimates of other people's deservedness. In other words, it is calling us to a kind of unlimited helpfulness, which responds only to need, without regard for anything else. Can you imagine what this would mean in our lives if we followed it? We would be following in the footsteps of the world's great examples of lovingkindness, people like Jesus, St. Francis, and Mother Teresa.

The Good Samaritan

A striking sequel to this sign occurred two months later. I was again preparing to lead a meeting of this same group. While pondering what to do, I had a sudden inspiration to compose a modern adaptation of Jesus' parable of the good Samaritan. By making the parable sound fresh and contemporary, I was hoping it would become a call to action for us, so that we would make our own small contribution to a more loving world.

In my retelling, I particularly wanted to capture a key feature of the parable that is lost on modern ears: the Jews hated Samaritans. To have a despised Samaritan *rescue* a Jew, especially after two fellow Jews had already passed him by, would have been a shocking twist for Jesus' Jewish audience. Such a twist could offend, but it could also puncture the balloon of ancient prejudice. It could open Jewish minds to the possibility that a *Samaritan* could be *good*.[18]

To reflect this feature, I told the story of a hate crime, in which the eventual rescuer was a member of the very group that had originally perpetrated the crime. My first thought was to make the victim a gay person, but I wanted to make the attackers skinheads and I didn't think that skinheads attacked gay people. Here, then, is my contemporary version of the good Samaritan:

> There was a young black man who had been out partying. When he was walking home he encountered some skinheads. The skinheads fell upon him and beat him to a pulp, leaving him half dead down an alley. Several people passed the alley and saw the man, but were either too scared or too uncon-cerned to check out how badly injured he was and offer help.
>
> But then another skinhead passed by, saw the young black man, and was moved to pity at the sight of him. He went up to him, carried him to his car, cleaned him up and bandaged his wounds, then drove him to the hospital. At the hospital he wait-ed several hours while they treated him. When informed he would have to stay for a few days, he gave them his address and told them to send the bill to his home.

While I was finishing this, I checked my e-mail. One of the messages that landed in my inbox was a petition for a federal law against hate crimes. The proposed law was inspired by the murder, a year earlier, of Matthew Shepard, a young gay man from Wyoming. On October 7, 1998, Shepard met two men in a bar and agreed to ride home with them. Shepard was then driven to a remote location, tied to a fence, savagely beaten, robbed, and left for dead. After eighteen hours in near-freezing temperatures, he was found by two passersby and taken to the hospital, where he died several days later.

The petition called for the passage of The Hate Crimes Prevention Act. It contained a resolution that affirmed "the inherent worth and dignity of every person," a theme that comes across so strongly in the parable of the good Samaritan.

The Matthew Shepard story struck me as something I had probably heard, but a year had passed and I couldn't quite be sure. Yet the parallels with my story were unmistakable. In both, there is a young man of minority persuasion who is out having a good time. On his way home he falls into the hands of people who hate members of his minority. They severely beat him and leave him for dead. He lies there for some time, but eventually a stranger (or strangers) finds him and he is taken to the hospital, where he remains for days. These already impressive parallels get slightly more impressive when you remember that I had initially wanted to make the young man in my story gay.

These similar stories were even being told for similar reasons. Both were meant to remind us that every person has worth and dignity, regardless of the group he or she belongs to. And both were the basis for a call to action, a call that is made to one or more members of my group (the petition, of course, came to me with a request to sign it), asking us to do our small part to contribute to a more loving, less hateful world.

The parable of the good Samaritan has gone down in history as one of the great images of human love and compassion. Here was a CMPE asking us to not just applaud this parable from a safe distance, but to make it contemporary and make it personal; to rise to its calling and live out its sublime counsel. The CMPE was also tapping into the parable's original thrust, which challenged the universal human tendency to restrict our love and kindness to our own group, reserving hate and attack for the outsider. The CMPE joined with the parable in calling us to not let our love stop at the boundaries of our group, but flow just as freely to those we would normally despise.

Here, in other words, was a CMPE calling us to live out the very highest in our nature.

Forgiveness

On a December morning in 2005, I was teaching a *Course in Miracles* class. When a woman named Linda began sharing at the end of the class, I realized she had just experienced a CMPE. While getting dressed before class, she had been mulling over a persistent issue with her weight. She realized that in all the losing and gaining, the real, underlying issue had never been addressed.

> And so I said to myself, there is something I am avoiding. The realization was that whatever I need to do...it will be the final resolution of what I call the "weight issue"....
> My awareness told me there was a "next step" that I really needed to take that I've never really honestly taken (or only half-heartedly taken) and then I proceeded to put on my eye make-up. As I was stroking the brush I literally heard "Forgiveness is what is next," and my response immediately was "No."
>
> At that moment, I knew I had to forgive to take the next step of my journey. Even though I practice forgiveness, there were four relationships where in my heart I had not forgiven *completely*; there was a tiny hold on not wanting to really let go and forgive. I feel the message was about my path itself, that if I wanted to move forward I needed to get the lesson full throttle. *Yet* I stood in front of that mirror saying "No," knowing what I was doing.

She then walked upstairs to my class (she was staying where the class was being held), having no clue what I was going to teach. I had chosen that morning to focus on a forgiveness exercise I had written, based on one of the lessons in the Course. Here is the exercise (with some redundant lines removed):

> Close your eyes. Think of your current life as if it's taking place inside of hell. Think of various problem areas in your life and see actual flames popping up in those places....Maybe you

are having financial difficulties. See flames coming out of your wallet or purse....Just think of various problem areas and see flames dancing in each of those areas.

Then, a little distance away, you see a massive, glorious door, the gate of Heaven....You walk toward it, and as you come nearer, you see it has a large keyhole, like you might see in a castle door....You find in your hand a large, old-fashioned key....You see that on it is engraved in beautiful writing the word "Forgiveness." Then you turn the key over, and on the other side it says, "of" and it gives a name. The name is someone you deeply need to forgive, but you have been putting it off. See whose name is there.

Realize that you have been refusing to use this key for a long time. If going through the gate means using this key, you are not sure it's worth it. Maybe the flames are preferable. How long have you been loitering here, in front of the gate, wondering if you should enter in and be at home?

You finally decide to forgive this person. Say to yourself, *"I let forgiveness rest upon [name], For thus forgiveness will be given me...."* [Repeat this several times.] Find that you have placed the key in the keyhole and are already turning it. You are forgiving this person at last. The key turns all the way and you pull the door open; it takes virtually no effort. As it swings open you find yourself face-to-face with a blazing light....The light of God....You are transfixed by this light, caught up in the ecstasy of it....You are home at last....Spend a few moments basking in this light.

Notice how parallel this was to Linda's train of thought right before class. In both cases, she goes through an inner process, which begins with her thinking about a surface problem or problems (her weight, her finances), but then moves on to the real issue. The process continues as a voice (an inner voice or my voice) tells her that this real issue is forgiveness. The understanding is given her that, in order to move forward (on her path, through the gate of Heaven), she needs to forgive. In particular, she needs to forgive a specific person or persons. She has been avoiding this step for a long time, unwilling to fully take it. Indeed, even now when she is faced with how imperative it is, she is not sure she wants to do it. (Linda said "no," and my exercise said, "You are not sure it's worth it.")

More than just being parallel, the two events were like bookends, with the first event representing the beginning of a process and the second the end. First, Linda hears a voice that says "Forgiveness is what is next," but she says "no." Then she is guided through my exercise, which openly acknowledges her "no," but asks her to say "yes" anyway. This had a profound effect on her:

Here I was so clearly being given the opportunity even after I had said "no." I hesitated, but…when you did the meditation, I said "yes" and did what I was told. I had put all four names on the key and kept repeating them until only my mother was left and then I knew who I was to start with….

I truly realized in that moment that forgiveness sets me free. I knew before your meditation that I was between a rock and a hard place, a stand-off between me and God. During the meditation that lifted. It felt like a near-death experience. In an NDE, a person goes to the light and is transformed. Your guided meditation took me to the light; I had a transforming experience. My life is different since that morning.

It is hard to escape the impression that the signs "wanted" Linda to have this breakthrough, that they wanted her to get past her resistance, forgive, and step into the light.

If we take this as a statement of the philosophy of the signs, then they are calling us to do one of the most sublime things we can do. When we forgive another, when we choose loving that person over hanging on to all the bumps and bruises of the past, we do one of the most beautiful things the human heart is capable of. Indeed, if the old saying is correct—"To err is human, to forgive divine"—then when we forgive, we reach beyond the merely human and partake in the divine.

Standing up, speaking out

The final CMPE is included here more for purposes of balance than anything else. The foregoing signs can easily give the impression that we should always meekly comply with the requests of others, no matter how outrageous they are. From these signs, we might easily conclude that when faced with wolves, we should always be gentle lambs.

This sign, however, tells another side of the story. In early 2004, Nicola had a counseling session with an astrologer, from which she took the following notes:

> Instead of running away from challenges, I need to stand up to them, and the people involved. I need to stand firm. I'm so obliging that people take advantage of me. I need to stand up for myself, not run away.
>
> My basic life challenge…is that I need to inject my insight and control into situations. I have great intuition and the power to make a real difference, and instead of seeing this as something that satisfies only my own needs [i.e., being worried that others will see it as this], I need to see it as something that benefits all concerned. I have this wisdom and intuition about things, and the power to make a real difference, and I must stand up for what I believe to be right in the face of people's opposition. At the end of the day it is not only for my best interests, but for everyone's.

In part, this was addressing Nicola's situation within the Circle, where she often had creative ideas to do things in new ways, yet hesitated to offer them. Since these ideas meant a break with the old, she feared she would encounter resistance, which in fact she often did. This resistance (intentionally or unintentionally) gave her the message that her ideas were designed to benefit the few rather than everyone. Hearing even a hint of this message would cause her to just shrink into the corner. It was therefore especially helpful for her to hear that her ideas stood to benefit everyone. The session as a whole, in fact, had an enormous effect on Nicola. It was a real turning point for her.

That same day, our friend Alexandra was at a transformational workshop. Part of that day's agenda was a game designed to show participants how they play the game of life. The participants were divided into two teams and each was given a question to answer.

During the game, a man on Alexandra's team spoke up and she immediately recognized that he had the right answer, even though no one was listening to him. She tried a few times to timidly speak up on his behalf. "But when nobody gave me the time of day," she said, "I surrendered. I gave up." She felt completely powerless to change the group's "lynch mob" mentality. Beforehand, she had assumed there would be many greater minds and that she could hang back and just let them handle it. Instead, she said, "All the loud voices were completely superficial and adversarial." And they just took over.

The game had accomplished its purpose. It had shown her how she lives her life. She saw how she typically plays small and stays silent, feeling, as she put it, "like I'm at the mercy of some amorphous group out there that somehow has it handled better than me." Now she realized she needed to speak up and make herself heard, because she is often genuinely in touch with what needs to happen. She felt this was especially relevant to her leadership role in the group mentioned earlier in "Service with a Smile" and "The Good Samaritan." (Interestingly, "Service with a Smile" approved of her doing exactly what she *didn't* do in this sign: bringing forth her idea in spite of the group's resistance.) She concluded, "I believe I have created all of this so that I could realize that I truly want to be an excellent leader."

The parallels between Nicola's session and Alexandra's game were obvious: The two of them are seeking help from a situation whose purpose is their growth. This situation leads them to a certain key realization. This realization applies to everything, but especially to their leadership role within the spiritual group or organization of which they are part. To fulfill that role, they must learn this lesson. They must learn that they too readily hang back, stay silent, and avoid confrontation, especially in a group. Instead, they need to be strong enough to speak up and inject their insight into the situation, regardless of the group's opposing voices. This is because they often have a wisdom and insight others don't have. They often know which way things are supposed to go, what is best for the group as a whole. This realization has a massive impact on them. It feels like the key that opens the door to the next phase of their lives.

This was an extraordinary set of parallels. How could two friends just happen to experience everything on this list on the same day?

This message of offering one's ideas in spite of opposing voices provides a useful balance, I think, to some of the earlier signs from this chapter. Those could easily give the impression that our role is to forever be the humble servant. Yet here we have a sign urging two people to do what looks like the exact opposite.

But is it really the opposite? If you think about it, this CMPE is really about how Nicola and Alexandra could fulfill their role *as* servant. It is about how they can fulfill their leadership role in a group dedicated to service. The ideas they are meant to put forth are ones that will benefit everyone in the group, as well as those served by the group. If they let dissenting voices silence them, these ideas will quite simply be unable to help the people they were meant to help.

This CMPE, then, is really not so different than the previous ones. It is not about being an eccentric rebel and telling everyone else to go to hell. It is about offering your help in spite of obstacles. Sometimes being truly helpful means giving your gift even when other voices are trying to shout you down.

A beautiful but challenging philosophy

It is not hard to sense an implicit philosophy running through these five CMPEs. They feel as if they are different applications of the same overall orientation. If we had to, we could condense that orientation into just two words: *toward others*. Slightly more expanded, we could express it this way:

> To go toward others with love and helpfulness, overlooking all
> that would normally hold us back.

Let's unpack this in several stages. To begin with, it is quite striking how often what "would normally hold us back" is featured in these signs. Indeed, in one form or another, it's there in all five of them. We have Peter being rude ("Laura's Special Function") and the Perrys being undeserving ("Service with a Smile"). We have the inbred hatred of those who are different ("The Good Samaritan"), the accumulation of past hurts ("Forgiveness"), and the opposition of strident voices ("Standing Up, Speaking Out"). Not a bad list of what causes us to withhold our love from others.

Our first need, therefore, is to experience an inner transformation, in which our emotional recoil from others is replaced with a genuine love for them. We need to reach a place where those qualities that would normally evoke hatred or callousness toward others no longer dictate our feelings toward them. We need to find a way to overlook those qualities. Like Linda, we need to find a way to forgive.

An inner transformation, however, is just the beginning. This needs to be followed up with outward helpfulness. We saw this theme again and again. We saw Laura making herself available to help Peter on the hotline, rather than staying home and avoiding him. We saw the group reaching out to help my family unpack, despite our questionable merit. We saw this same group being called to live out the message of the good Samaritan, one of history's immortal images of selfless generosity. And we saw Nicola and Alexandra being told to speak up, rather than clam up, when they had an insight that could benefit everyone.

This outward helpfulness often took a particular form that was the "special function" of the helper. This, of course, was a major theme in "Laura's Special Function." It was also present in the final CMPE, "Standing Up, Speaking Out," which was about how Alexandra could carry out her special function in she group she leads, and about how Nicola could carry out her function within the Circle of Atonement.

Yet "overlooking all that would normally hold us back" is not what humans naturally do. And so we find nearly every one of these CMPEs pervaded by *resistance*. Laura questioned going back to the crisis center. The group questioned helping the Perrys unpack. Linda initially said "no" to forgiveness. Alexandra and Nicola were tempted to withhold their gift, rather than risk confrontation with the group. Even while we hear the call to reach out to others, we also feel the stubborn pull of our comfort zone.

Clearly, these five CMPEs are cut from the same cloth. But are they representative of CMPEs as a whole? In my experience, they are. Indeed, you can see what I mean just by glancing through the other examples in the book. The signs about my writing (Chapter 7) fit this pattern to a T. Writing is a central aspect of my own special function, and in this function, the signs said I need to resist the temptation to back off from my audience and instead step forward toward them.

The CMPEs about Steve (Chapter 9) also fit this pattern. They were all about him resisting the temptation to withdraw from others into a fantasy world, and instead serving and joining with the people in his life now. They pictured him doing that in the special function of pastoral counseling he was preparing for.

I could continue going through other examples in the book, but you get my point. CMPEs do appear to have an overall philosophy. As I said earlier, this in itself is noteworthy. Why on earth would we expect a series of completely random events to express a consistent system of values? How can randomness be consistent? Better yet, how can the consistency we see here be random?

What do we make of this philosophy? First of all, I believe there is a real beauty to it. One of the most deeply inspiring things on this earth is when one person sincerely reaches out to another in spite of what normally holds people back, overlooking the other's abuse, disregarding ethnic divides, and letting go of the awful weight of the past. Stories about this are some of the most beloved stories in our culture. Think of the good Samaritan. The people who really do this become some of the most revered figures in history. You can think of their names yourself. There is something deep in the race that yearns for this.

And yet there is also something deep in us that resists it. It is inspiring to watch, but when it comes to doing it ourselves, it feels like our feet are planted in concrete. Therefore, in addition to being beautiful, this philosophy is also extremely challenging. It calls us out of our self-centeredness. It asks us to emerge from the entrenched comfort zone we never thought to leave.

Whether you agree or disagree with this philosophy, whether you want to argue with it or follow it, I do think it naturally compels respect. The signs are not taking the easy road; they are taking the high road. They are calling us to our highest potential, the potential to embody a pure and uncommon goodness. And if they call us to the highest within us, what does that say about where they themselves come from?

Chapter 11
Physical Evidence for a God Who Cares

Full Circle

By August 1999, I had become deeply impressed with the signs. It had gradually dawned on me that they had importance for more than just me. As a result, I began thinking about writing a book to share what I had found.

A month before this, I had also met my future wife Nicola. We had struck up a lively e-mail correspondence, and I decided it was time I introduced her to this phenomenon that was so central to my life. So one evening I sat down and wrote her a fourteen-page summary of what signs are and how they work. It was the first time I had committed the entire model to paper. Near the end I shared with her my sense of the significance of this phenomenon and my plans to write a book about it:

The potential importance of the signs
I really believe that what I've discovered about signs…has great potential importance….The Western world has largely outgrown notions of a universe in which there is a Mind that has a plan for our lives, that cares about us, that looks out for us, that wants our happiness, and that arranges events…to obtain its objectives. That is all the stuff of fairy tales, of religious mythology. We have become disenchanted with that sort of thing as we have become enchanted with applying our intellects to the physical world.

What is so great about these signs is that they are a coming together of both of these worlds. On the one hand, they apply our intellect to the data of the physical world. On the other hand, this yields concrete evidence of a divine plan at work in our lives, a plan that cares, that wants our happiness, that has definite objectives. It is an absolutely wild combination. It is almost like aiming a massive telescope up at the stars and seeing Santa's sled racing across the sky. The signs make the statement that when you get really rational and objective and willing to look at the evidence, you come full circle and return to a view in which a loving God has a plan to save the world.

So someday I plan to publish what I have learned....I want to get something started. There is a plan, and there is a way to touch that plan and know what it is.

A few sentences after this, I took a break to join my family in front of the TV. As I watched the program they had on, I was amazed at what I saw. It connected so intimately with what I had just written that I knew it had to be a sign. The next morning, I inserted a report into that same piece I was writing for Nicola:

A sign about this paper

Hey, guess what? I just had a sign about what I wrote! It happened a few sentences after this point, but the sign was about the preceding three paragraphs, so I'll insert the story here. Now you get to see how the whole thing works. Isn't this exciting? [Interestingly, here was my first example of a sign showing the reader "how the whole thing works."]

OK, here's what happened. After adding a few paragraphs to this rather long piece I went upstairs to join the family for a few minutes in front of the TV before going to bed....They were watching...*The X-Files*....

[The episode] focuses on Scully, the female partner. She is the epitome of rational scientific skepticism. In every show she offers a scientific explanation for the paranormal things that she and Mulder are investigating. She only believes in what she can see and touch and verify scientifically. Because of this rational scientific bent [I assumed] she has left the Catholic faith of her childhood behind.

But this show is really about her experiencing a kind of return to that faith. A line keeps cropping up in the show, which is about the case they are working on but also about Scully: Sometimes you have to come full circle to find the truth. And that is what happens to her in this episode. She is guarding a young boy who is a stigmatist. He, it turns out, is believed by some evil guy to be important for the future of the world. The bad guy is stalking him and trying to kill him. Various miraculous things happen while Scully is guarding him. [In addition to bearing the wounds of the stigmata, the boy bilocates, and the dead body of his guardian emits a smell of flowers, like the bodies of incorruptible saints.] It even seems that Scully has been chosen by the powers that be to be his guardian.

She is deeply affected by the miracles she witnesses. At the end of the show she goes to a Catholic priest for confession to talk about these things. She explains that she left the Church a long time ago, but that she has witnessed miracles and now she is wondering about returning. She is then shocked to hear the Father say the line that has woven throughout the show: "Sometimes you have to come full circle to find the truth." She is shaken and he asks her how she feels. She says it makes her afraid, "afraid that God is speaking and no one is listening." That's the last line of the show.

I recently viewed this episode (titled "Revelations"). Here are its final lines:

PRIEST: Perhaps you saw these things because you needed to.
SCULLY: To find my way back?
PRIEST: Sometimes we must come full circle to find the truth. [Upon hearing this line again, Scully is startled and looks up at the priest.] Why does that surprise you?
SCULLY: Mostly, it just makes me afraid.

PRIEST: Afraid?

SCULLY: Afraid that God is speaking...but that no one's listening.

That last line stayed with me. It wasn't entirely clear why Scully said it, but it conjured an image of miracles occurring all over yet somehow being overlooked or dismissed, perhaps by the same skeptical mindset that had dominated her own outlook. And so, sadly, God's voice was falling on a world of deaf ears. This image struck a real chord with me. In the symbolism of the sign, it seemed intended as a description of the predicament of the signs. Could it be that, in the form of CMPEs, God is speaking, yet no one is listening?

Returning to my paper to Nicola, I then began to process the sign:

The parallels between what I wrote [event 1] and this episode [event 2] were very striking to me. In interpreting a sign, I'll usually list such parallels like this:

- Both talked about a rational scientific mindset that believes only what the intellect can prove based on physical evidence.
- In both, that rational scientific mindset had left behind a traditional religious faith in a loving God who is speaking to the world.
- Both spoke about that mindset witnessing physical events that required a spiritual explanation, and therefore had the power to bring this mindset back to its traditional faith in some sense.
- Amazingly, both used the phrase "coming full circle" to express this return to a traditional faith in God speaking to the world.

In other words, Scully played the role of the Western world

from my above paragraph. The stigmatist kid played the role of the signs, providing physical evidence for a spiritual worldview....

I usually try to boil the meaning of a sign down into a single paragraph, maybe two. So here is my interpretation:

"The signs are a situation in which, when you apply the intellect to a certain body of physical evidence, you obtain evidence of a loving God Who has a plan for the world. By employing the same mindset that has brought our Western world away from faith in a loving God, the signs have the potential to bring people full circle. They really do have potential importance for our world. It is therefore a good idea for me to write a book about them and try to have it reach a large number of people."

Now, usually, such a sign will connect with a whole tapestry of past signs. But this one is expressing virtually a brand new theme....So this is kind of exciting to have a new theme crop up.

This CMPE left a deep impression on me. It said that signs are a case of God speaking, and doing so in such a tangible, verifiable way that they could help heal our painful split between science and religion. From this point on, I became serious about writing this book.

As I look back on this occurrence, I realize that it foreshadowed so much. Since this was the first time I put the model down on paper for someone else, it was really a foreshadowing of writing this book. And since that someone else turned out to be my future partner in the signs, it also foreshadowed that partnership. Finally, since other signs eventually did follow in the footsteps of this one, it foreshadowed them as well. This may have been the first CMPE to announce these themes, but as we'll see later, it wasn't the last.

CMPEs are a truly remarkable phenomenon. I don't know of anything quite like them. Now that we have learned the basic contours of this phenomenon and seen how it behaves, we have an opportunity to stand back and assess it. How can we explain the existence of CMPEs? Where do they come from? This chapter will attempt to answer these questions.

In trying to answer them, I am making a crucial assumption, that my experience of CMPEs thus far will hold true on a wider basis. I don't have any reason to believe this will not be the case. At this point, I know many people who have had their own CMPEs, and theirs look exactly like mine. Further, I do run across the occasional CMPE in the literature on synchronicity. Based on my experience, I personally cannot imagine that this phenomenon isn't happening all over, and that people simply lack the concept that would illuminate its occurrence.

However, until this has been actually verified, we obviously need to treat the whole matter, including my speculations below, as provisional. My purpose here is to simply open the book on this phenomenon, to have the *first* word on it, not the last. I am still learning about it, and I fully expect that in time my rendering of the model will be greatly improved upon. Yet however imperfectly I have described it, this is a real phenomenon, one that merits further investigation.

Not random

To begin with, we need to admit that in a universe that is fundamentally mindless and purposeless, CMPEs as I have described them could not exist. I have made this argument in pieces throughout the book, but I will summarize it here.

First, the events that constitute a CMPE do not have just one thing in common, as we typically expect from a conventional synchronicity. Instead, the events of a CMPE have on average a list of eight things in common. This list of parallels contains highly improbable elements and captures central features of each event. Further, it tells a single story, because both events contain the same essential story—the same basic parts connected in the same basic ways. Such an integrated constellation of parallels is very difficult to explain as the product of chance.

Second, CMPEs tend to aim their focus at situations that are significant to us personally, situations about which we feel unresolved and need counsel. They give every appearance of being *responsive*, of addressing things that matter to us. If signs were merely random, the things they focused on would of course be random as well. But they aren't.

Third, CMPEs are structured in such a way as to offer a perspective on the situations they address. A frequent way they do this is to lay next to our situation another situation that is strikingly parallel, but not in all ways. This "symbolic situation" often contains key differences, and these differences seem designed to *answer* our need for resolution and for counsel. These differences can even offer predictions. For instance, in the Dead Sea Scrolls sign (Chapter 8), the symbolic situation contained the "guerrilla" release of the Dead Sea Scrolls, which had no parallel in the sign's other event. As we saw, this difference ended up conveying an accurate prediction of the future of *A Course in Miracles*. The random hypothesis has a hard enough time explaining the parallels. Can it also explain these well-placed differences?

Fourth, in all of this, CMPEs consistently display the same specific structure. I have described this structure using four main points, with each point having several sub-points. (This might be a good time to review my summary of the model on page 86). A genuine sign will always contain all four points and all or almost all of the sub-points. In other words, what we have here is a very consistent phenomenon. If CMPEs are random events, why do they keep following the same detailed pattern?

Fifth, different CMPEs are extraordinarily interrelated. They address the same situations and in doing so convey consistent messages, often have a similar form (similar events, symbols, and lists of parallels), and sometimes even occur on the same date in different years. If the previous points had strained a chance explanation, this one demolishes it.

Sixth, CMPEs don't just convey messages; they appear to give *high-quality* messages, which can see far into the future, see deeply into people and situations, and offer practical, effective advice. We all know it is much easier to give bad advice than good. Can we realistically expect that *random* advice would be any good at all?

Seventh, CMPEs appear to have a philosophy; they demonstrate a consistent system of values. This philosophy seems to aim at the actualizing of our highest potentials. It constantly beckons us toward the attainment of a radical goodness. How does something like that emerge from a series of random occurrences?

Looking over these seven characteristics, do we actually believe this phenomenon can be explained away as the product of mere chance? I am the first to admit that a chance explanation works well for most standard coincidences. But it utterly fails with CMPEs. It starts failing at the second point in the model, the parallels, and from there the failures just compound. As I said before, this is a real phenomenon, and we need to deal with it as such.

Are people unconsciously arranging similar events to happen together?

Another possible explanation for these occurrences is that there *is* more going on here than chance, but that this "more" is simply the unconscious behavior of the people involved. In this scenario, the first event unconsciously influences the person involved to cause a second event to occur that is similar. Or knowledge that the second event is *going* to occur influences the person to cause a similar *first* event to occur. For example, with "Full Circle" (beginning of this chapter), maybe I went to watch that *X-Files* episode (event 2) because I knew it was on and knew that its themes were similar to what I had just written (event 1). Or maybe I knew ahead of time that my family was going to watch it, and that inspired me to write what I did in event 1. This explanation, in other words, claims that the events are never *truly* independent (going back to my discussion of independence in Chapter 3).

It is reasonable to raise this question with many CMPEs, but most end up being immune to this explanation. For instance, with "Full Circle," I hadn't the slightest idea what my family was watching. No sound could reach me from the TV, as I was tucked away in the basement while the television was upstairs, at the opposite end of a large house. For many CMPEs, event 2 happens without any cooperation whatsoever from the person involved in event 1. This was true of "Standing up, Speaking out" (Chapter 10), the sign right before "Full Circle." There, Alexandra and Nicola had no influence on or knowledge of what was happening to the other that day.

As I said, most CMPEs are like these two. If the stories being told are basically accurate, we cannot explain this phenomenon as a case of the people involved unconsciously influencing the events to be similar.

Are the stories accurate?

In my mind, the best skeptical explanation is to say that we have no way of knowing if the stories are in fact accurate. This is a reasonable response. As the one telling these stories, I could, after all, be perpetrating a hoax. Even assuming my essential goodwill, I could be telling stories based on hazy memory, or embellishing stories for dramatic effect.

On the memory front, I will say that I do write down the events soon after and check them with others if need be. Further, the overwhelming majority of my signs have at least one event that is either written (such as an article or e-mail) or is recorded on audio or video (such as a movie or TV program). This significantly reduces reliance on memory. In many signs, *both* events are written or recorded, which means that memory plays no role at all, and these signs are just as strong as the others. In fact, we have seen twelve such signs so far in this book (the first being "The How-to Component" in Chapter 1 and the last being "Full Circle" at the beginning of this chapter).

On the embellishment front, let me assure you I have not embellished these stories. I have not employed dramatic license. I have been very careful to refrain from exaggeration. To the best of my knowledge, every detail of the stories I have told is accurate.

Yet, of course, you as the reader cannot really be sure of that. This is one of the reasons it is imperative that examples of this phenomenon be widely recorded and by people other than myself. Once that is done, I am confident the accuracy question will be put to rest.

An apparent communication

If we acknowledge this as a real phenomenon and deal with it on its own terms, what do its characteristics suggest about what it is? As I have said before, in every way this phenomenon looks like a communication. To see what I mean, we can go through its characteristics and see the impression they tend to make on our minds.

What we first notice about a CMPE is that events have spontaneously come together that have an uncanny amount in common. The psychological effect of this is to stop us in our tracks and say to us, "Pay attention. Don't treat this as the usual randomness of life. There is an intelligence at work here."

Then, when we pay attention, we notice that a situation in our life is being addressed, usually one in which we feel a need for answers. This gives us the feeling that whatever intelligence might be at work here, it is not unmindful of our concerns. Rather, it seems to be actually *responding* to our concerns.

As we look further, we realize this confluence of events conveys a particular *perspective* on our situation. The situation is being cast in a certain light, framed in a certain way. And this way of framing it seems to actually provide the answers we were looking for.

The impression we get, in other words, is that something is shaping ordinary events into a message, a message aimed at a situation we need help with. It looks like something is trying to get a point across to us. It looks like a *communication*.

This impression increases as we note that the message doesn't seem random and mindless, but rather seems quite intelligent. It seems to really see into the situation, perhaps even into its future. And if there is concrete advice offered, that advice may prove quite effective. This overall intelligence of the message just heightens the feeling that this is a real communication, not just the turning of mindless gears.

Further, the message has the hallmarks of *intent*. It is not some dry, value-neutral observation of the facts. Rather, it contains value judgments. It contains goals. It points out the right way and the wrong way, and seems to actually be pulling us toward the former and away from the latter. In short, it appears to be soaked with intention and purpose—which again strengthens our feeling that this is an actual communication.

This feeling is reinforced one last time as additional CMPEs repeatedly address this same situation and even say consistent things about it. This conjures in our minds a picture of the various CMPEs issuing from a single mindset, one that holds steady over time. Indeed, we see that CMPEs even display a consistent overall system of values. This, of course, is exactly how we experience normal communication, where a particular communicator will tend to talk about the same subjects over time and say much the same things about them, as a reflection of his basic value system.

As you can see, all of the characteristics of this phenomenon convey the impression that there is some sort of intelligence or mindfulness at work here, one that is trying to get a message across to us. The more you experience this phenomenon and understand its workings, the more unmistakable this impression becomes. Speaking for myself, after hundreds of CMPEs, I cannot doubt that something is communicating with me, any more than you can doubt that other people are communicating with you.

Yet this, of course, does not prove that it is so. All I have described here are what CMPEs *appear* to be, what *impression* they make on our minds. That doesn't mean this is what they *are*. What it does mean, however, is that their characteristics are immediately suggestive of them being a communication. And it means these characteristics will have to be accounted for by any explanation we offer. If a hypothesis claims CMPEs are not a communication, it will still have to plausibly account for these same characteristics. It will have to explain how they can be there in the absence of a communication taking place.

What follows are the three explanations I can think of that most fully and plausibly account for the characteristics of this phenomenon. The first one does not include the idea of communication, while the second two do.

Explanation #1: Similar events cluster in time and space according to some unknown law, probably something to do with quantum physics.

The most visible aspect of this phenomenon is events that are improbably similar unintentionally coming together in time. One possible explanation, therefore, is that there is some undiscovered law by which similar events are *attracted* to each other. This attraction draws them closer together and occasionally succeeds in getting them to collide in time and space. In this view, their collision doesn't mean anything, just as an apple being attracted to the Earth by gravity doesn't mean anything. It is just the workings of a natural law.

Such a hypothesis, of course, would go way beyond current science. To even vaguely justify it, we would no doubt invoke quantum physics, which is being used these days to justify all sorts of paranormal and spiritual things (sometimes credibly and sometimes not-so-credibly). But in doing so, at least we could stay arguably within the basic scientific worldview in which things happen according to mindless, impersonal forces, rather than because invisible spirits are running around messing with reality.

Attractive as this is, it explains only the first two points of the model: events and parallels. It explains only events coming together that are extremely parallel. I think, though, we could possibly stretch it a bit more. Let's add in the idea that the energy of our concern about a particular situation is what draws together events, events that parallel the situation we are concerned about. This more or less allows us to also explain the model's third point: the subject situation. As we have seen, the events of a sign always involve or at least parallel some situation of relevance to us, a situation we are usually concerned about.

However, when we hit the fourth point of the model—interpretation— we run into a big problem. The problem is not that there would be no interpretation. Even if events were drawn together by some sort of impersonal law, we could still take away from the experience some sort of message. For instance, if after our discussion of forming a bucket brigade (Chapter 1), we had happened to encounter a negative story about a bucket brigade, we would have interpreted the sign as saying, "*Don't* form a bucket brigade."

The real problem is that the message would just be a random byproduct of a mindless process. It would not be intended by the CMPE itself. There would thus be nothing crafting it to make sure it was a high-quality message. Rather, it would be completely random. It would be a roll of the dice.

As a result, all that we have seen in the previous four chapters would not exist. There would be no reason that messages from different signs would be consistent (Chapter 7). Each time a CMPE spoke to a particular situation, it would be a new roll of the dice. There would be no reason to have accurate predictions (Chapter 8). Any prediction that seemed to be made would again be just a roll of the dice. There would be no reason CMPEs would display deep and accurate insight into a person or situation, or give effective practical advice (Chapter 9). And there would certainly be no reason they would display a consistent philosophy (Chapter 10). Such a thing does not emerge from rolling dice.

Without something intelligent guiding the messages of CMPEs, those messages would be random, resulting in utter chaos on the message level. This, as you have seen, is not what we find with this phenomenon. And I can guarantee you that if tomorrow it switched over to this, to complete chaos on the message level, I would notice. The phenomenon would suddenly be fundamentally different. I would lose everything I value about it, including all motivation to write this book.

So while this hypothesis is a good attempt at explaining the phenomenon, it doesn't go far enough. The reason is that by appealing to impersonal law, it tries to get mindless randomness to do the work only an intelligent mind can do. It takes a mind to craft an insightful, accurate, practical, prescient, and consistent message. Mindless mechanism just can't do that. Even if one day computers will be able to do that, it will still have taken a great many intelligent minds to *program* those computers.

I don't see, therefore, how we can explain this phenomenon without invoking mind. Of course, if we decide that only certain of its characteristics *need* explaining, we can probably explain it without mind. But then we won't be explaining *it*, but rather our own cherry-picked version of it. If we take the whole thing, just as it is, then in my view we have no choice but to explain it as communication from some sort of mind. This brings us to our final two explanations.

Explanation #2: CMPEs are a physical manifestation of some wise element in our unconscious.

If CMPEs are communications, who is the sender? Unlike most communications, CMPEs have no obvious sender. They appear to be completely anonymous—like some sort of benign cosmic ransom note.

The current explanation posits that the sender is our own unconscious mind—that there is some wise element in our unconscious that actually has power to directly bend and shape the physical world, and thereby "dream" messages into our lives, just as it can embed messages in our nighttime dreams.

Once you believe in the unconscious and in paranormal abilities, which most of us do, this is not so far-fetched. For instance, paranormal investigators have observed that poltergeist phenomena—where a house or workplace experiences such things as moving objects, shaking beds, and loud thumps and raps—are usually focused around a particular *living* person, often a troubled teenager. The frequent conclusion is that psychic energy is shooting out of this teen's mind (along with all the other things that shoot out of a teen's mind) and disrupting the physical environment. Perhaps CMPEs are a less chaotic, more controlled version of the same principle. Perhaps there is some wise element in our mind that impresses its message onto the fabric of time and space through the use of paranormal powers.

I personally think this is a reasonable hypothesis, one that accounts for at least most of the evidence at hand. Indeed, it is what I myself used to assume about this phenomenon.

However, as I began to work with more than just my own signs, I gradually noticed a major problem with this hypothesis: I was unable to detect the signs of different individuals having anything individual about them, any kind of individual cast or color. If my signs are coming from my unconscious and your signs are coming from yours, then presumably my signs will reflect the unique contours of my unconscious, and your signs will reflect the unique contours of yours. Consequently, my signs and your signs will say different things and say them in different ways. It's even reasonable to assume they will sometimes say directly opposite things.

This is certainly what we find with internal guidance. When I sit down with a group and we all seek inner guidance on the same question, there will often be an impressive accord between what different ones of us receive. Sometimes two of us will even get the same phrase or sentence. But there will often be differences. These include the inevitable differences in manner of expression as well as the more weighty differences in what the messages say.

Yet I have never noticed this with CMPEs. Instead, I have noticed just the opposite. From all that I can see, it doesn't matter to whom a sign happens. If it comments on the same situation other signs have commented on, what it says will be consistent with those signs, often remarkably so.

We have already seen examples of this. For instance, in Chapter 9 we saw six signs about Steve. Most of them happened to Steve, but one of them happened to me. Yet they clearly all expressed the same detailed point of view. I regularly find this when I receive signs about people I'm trying to help. The signs that come to me and the signs that come to them are indistinguishable.

As another example, a number of signs have affirmed the value of Nicola's ideas, especially about problem-solving within situations. We have seen several examples of this (including "The Bucket Brigade" in Chapter 1, "Family Comes First" in Chapter 4, and "Two Fundraising Letters" in Chapter 7). A number of such signs have come to Nicola herself, such as "Standing up, Speaking out" from the previous chapter, which explicitly told her she has valuable ideas to offer and should not be afraid to offer them.

Yet this same theme showed up in signs that happened to me and were for me. In Chapter 7, I reviewed three signs about my writing. All three of them backed up Nicola's advice for how I could resolve a dilemma with my writing. Even though they were my signs and she just played a cameo role, she showed up totally "in character," in exactly the same way she was portrayed in her own signs.

These are just brief snapshots of an across-the-board characteristic of CMPEs. As far as I can tell, signs express the same viewpoints regardless of to whom they come. As we have seen, signs coming to different people will portray particular individuals in the same way. They will also portray particular situations in the same way. For instance, with signs about the Circle of Atonement, it doesn't matter if signs come to me, Nicola, Greg, our other two board members, or even our staff members. All of them fit seamlessly together, like different pieces of a jigsaw puzzle. This even extends beyond the board and staff. One of our students had a massive five-event sign about a retreat center for the Circle, which featured the symbol of "the little garden." This woman had no idea that for years we had been receiving similar signs featuring that symbol (as you saw in Chapter 7). This sign even happened on the exact same date that, the year before, Nicola and I had received another sign about a property for the Circle.

This consistency between different people's signs clearly weakens the hypothesis under discussion. The fact that signs freely roam across the boundaries between people while retaining a unified outlook suggests they come from a unified place. It suggests that my signs are not being generated by the unique contours of my unconscious mind, but rather by something that transcends my personal mind.

As a result, this hypothesis loses what would have been its major rationale. What reason do we have now to claim that a person's signs come from that person's unconscious?

We could potentially save this hypothesis, but only with major surgery. To do so, we would have to posit that my CMPEs are coming from a place in my unconscious mind that is at one with all other unconscious minds, or at least in very close concert with them, so that all these minds speak with a single voice.

To really make this hypothesis work, we would also have to ascribe additional qualities to this unified unconscious. We would have to say that it is extremely consistent over time (Chapter 7), that it can see into the future (Chapter 8), that it can see deeply into situations and offer wise counsel (Chapter 9), and that it promotes a consistent set of higher values (Chapter 10).

But then, in fashioning this notion of a collective, wise, prescient, insightful, ethical, and psychically powerful unconscious, we have really fashioned a notion of God, haven't we? At this point, then, we are just avoiding the obvious. We are jumping through hoops to get around saying the word "God." Which brings us to our final category.

Explanation #3: CMPEs in some sense come from God.

I have mostly refrained from using the "G" word up until now. The reason is that I didn't want to convey the impression that this phenomenon depends on prior religious faith. It clearly doesn't. It is a phenomenon in its own right, one that happens naturally, without our cooperation, and happens to believers and non-believers alike. I especially didn't want to convey that the whole thing is just some tortured attempt to cook up evidence for God. I personally find such attempts unappetizing.

I offer the current explanation for the simple reason that the phenomenon itself pushes us in this direction. That is exactly what has happened to us in this chapter. We have only been pushed to this highest rung on the ladder because all the lower rungs failed. We first saw the random hypothesis and the unconscious influence hypothesis fail. We then went up from there to the hypothesis that some impersonal law of quantum physics was causing similar events to be attracted to each other. When this failed to account for the evidence, we were forced to consider more extreme explanations, involving some sort of mind communicating with us. The most modest version of this was the idea that our own unconscious mind was "dreaming" messages into our waking reality. Yet the evidence forced us to modify this hypothesis until we had created a notion of the unconscious that was obviously God-like. And that, of course, deposited us where we are now.

Once you step back and survey the phenomenon as a whole, it is hard not to think of God. We have seen a phenomenon in which events converge in ways that are so incredibly improbable that chance seems out of the question. Rather, it appears as if some unseen presence is mysteriously orchestrating events so as to shape them into a message for us. This presence seems responsive to our needs, since it speaks to situations in which we need counsel. By giving us this counsel, it displays the characteristics one would associate with a counselor, a guide, or a parent.

It seems to have our welfare in mind, since it apparently tries to move us in the direction of achieving successful outcomes and realizing our own highest potentials. In trying to move us in these directions, it treats the details as secondary, staying instead utterly focused on its big picture, its overall plan for our lives. This plan seems to be woven together with its plan for other lives, thus suggesting that all are part of some grand plan. The essence of this plan is our realization of some of the highest values humanity has known, values in which, above all, we need to go toward others with love and helpfulness in spite of all that would normally hold us back. This plan, in other words, asks us to follow in the footsteps of history's greatest spiritual exemplars.

Maybe you can read that without thinking of God, but I can't. In light of the characteristics of CMPEs as I have observed them—and assuming those characteristics hold true on a wider basis—the idea that they in some sense come from God is the best explanation I am aware of. (I say "in some sense" in order to leave room for the intermediaries that so many traditions and teachings speak of—such as the Holy Spirit and angels.)

God certainly isn't the only explanation. CMPEs could be the product of some incredibly advanced alien race that can control physical events without us seeing the strings being pulled. They could be the product of the devil—though it would be a strange devil that tries to influence us in such saintly directions. Or as I said earlier, they could be the product of some global committee of our own unconscious minds. For now, though, the evidence is so directly suggestive of God that, until evidence comes along that justifies jumping over to a less natural explanation, I will stick with this one.

As I mentioned earlier, this is not where I started out. Early on, I had no clear idea of where CMPEs were coming from. Actually, I didn't really even ask the question. My emphasis was far more utilitarian. I wanted guidance for my life and CMPEs appeared to know more than I did. Later, I assumed that some element in my unconscious was sending me signals about the plan for my life. Finally, about twenty years down the road, the nature of the phenomenon itself had gradually nudged me in the direction of seeing God as its source.

Part of what can make this explanation difficult to entertain is that it just seems too good to be true. We have been conditioned to believe there will never be hard evidence for God, that even if such evidence should miraculously appear, it will always vanish before the guys in the lab coats show up. We have thus concluded that belief must remain a private matter of the heart, a serene conviction that sees the facts, but knows better. The entire modern mood, the whole uneasy truce between science and religion, says that actual physical, publicly observable evidence for God will never exist—and that we shouldn't need it anyway.

Yet what if such evidence *did* show up, and the guys in the lab coats *could* investigate it? CMPEs are so physical, so publicly observable that many people could take the journey I have taken. If you are of a more skeptical bent, imagine that one day soon you experience a conjunction of events that fits to a T the model in this book. When you process it according to the rules here, you find it actually offers what seems like sound advice. Of course, one such event is not going to shake your worldview, but then imagine that you have additional experiences just like the first. Perhaps you begin recording them, just as an intellectual curiosity. Then imagine you start seeing connections between them. You see them addressing a certain situation repeatedly and, amazingly, saying the same things about it.

Let's say that after a couple of years of this, you have a new CMPE that is strikingly reminiscent of an old one, and then you look up the old one and find that it happened on the exact same date, and chills go down your spine as you stare in disbelief at the date. Finally, let's say that experience slowly drags you into actually trusting the signs, into treating them as a valued counselor in your life. At some point along this progression, I predict you will not be able to authentically shake the feeling that something is speaking to you and trying to guide you. At some point along the way, I predict this phenomenon will become so real, so reliable, so trusted, that if your worldview stands in its way, your worldview will fall.

There is something deeply convincing about the experience of CMPEs. It's one thing to hear about someone else's sign, but it's quite another to experience one yourself. The sheer improbability of the events is what hits you at first. You instinctively feel that this wasn't just chance.

Yet in the end, I think what leaves an even deeper impression is the wisdom contained therein. I have come to believe that one of the properties of mind is that it recognizes when it's in the presence of a greater mind. Mind knows when it encounters more of itself. Even when we aren't conscious of it or won't admit it, somewhere inside we know when a larger mind is in the room. I have heard, for instance, that killer whales perform, not for food, but for the love of their trainers. Somehow, in those tiny creatures that they could easily crush, the whales sense the presence of a greater mind, and they seek the love and attention of that mind. In this sense, I feel like the whale—I recognize in CMPEs the presence of a larger mind. I don't always like what they have to say, but I feel that somehow, they are seeing right inside me while at the same time surveying things from a great height. And I see others around me respond to this same quality.

In my experience, then, the belief that CMPEs come from God is not a credulous and superstitious reaction to flashy events. It is a feeling that grows in one through long and repeated contact, a feeling that doesn't need the support of religious belief systems, a feeling that one may never even articulate to oneself, but that is simply an innate response to the presence of a greater mind.

The Signs Weigh in

Now let's turn to what the signs themselves claim about their origin. What we find is the same conclusion we were brought to by examining their characteristics. Signs claim that they come from God. We saw this in "Full Circle," the CMPE with which I opened the chapter. It was the first sign I had that announced this theme, but since then there have been others.

Science to Discover God's Plan

In April 2002, I was working on an initial outline for this book. Naturally, I wove into my outline the themes of the "Full Circle" sign from three years earlier. Here are notes I wrote down for the introduction:

> **A phenomenon both natural and difficult for the modern mindset**
> It accommodates our modern mindset—it is publicly observable events.
> It is highly problematic to our modern mindset—because they appear to be the workings of a higher mind impressing itself on the stuff of time and space

And these are notes for the planned final chapter, "Physical evidence for a plan that cares" (which became the chapter you are reading now):

In a random world, this would not happen
I don't see a way to explain these events other than by virtue of a God who cares.

That same day I was sent the following e-mail, which seemed almost like a mirror image of what I had been writing:

$1 Million for Science to Discover God's Plan

Can science divine the hand of God in the universe?

Investment tycoon Sir John Templeton wants to know, and he's paying a total of $1 million to 15 scientists to look for a purpose in the cosmos....The money gives the opportunity to focus on the question that intrigues Templeton...: Is the universe the product of design or accident?..."Is there a fundamental purpose in the cosmos?"

...Those who received a piece of the money say it is freeing them up to explore ideas that wouldn't be supported by government funding because they touch on philosophy and religion. And while $1 million is small money for science, it can support a number of theorists developing unconventional ideas.

The Templeton Foundation is not without its critics in science. Nobel-winning physicist Steven Weinberg of the University of Texas has denounced attempts to make science and religion compatible.

The parallels were not hard to see. In both cases, there is an investigation in progress that hopes to break a new and important discovery to the world (in terms of event 2, what could be more important than science discovering God's plan?). It is about finding physical evidence for "God's plan" (in event 1, "a plan that cares" obviously referred to God's plan). This investigation, then, represents a kind of marriage of the scientific spirit with the religious worldview (the very marriage denounced by Steven Weinberg in event 2).

Since the subject situation was clearly the book I was working on, the sign was applying all that to this book. It was saying, in other words, that this book represented that important discovery of physical evidence for God's plan, a discovery that marries the scientific spirit with the religious worldview.

What really amazed me was that everything it said had also been said in the original sign, "Full Circle." Here I was following that original sign's counsel—writing the book it had told me to write and including in it the themes it had announced—and while I was doing that, another sign came along that said the very same things.

I haven't had any other CMPEs that stated these themes this directly. However, I have had three additional signs about the writing of this book, all of which you have seen. If we look closely at those signs, you will be surprised (or maybe you won't by this point!) to see some of the same themes lurking in their background.

The How-to Component of this Book

The first was "The How-to Component of this Book" (Chapter 1). Its main focus was confirming one of the purposes of this book: to provide instruction in how to work with your own signs. However, as a secondary focus, it also confirmed the book's *other* purpose as expressed in this paragraph:

> I am trying to fulfill two purposes in writing this book. The first is to make this phenomenon known. This is a real phenomenon. It deserves to be studied. It deserves to be in the public eye. Its implications are potentially revolutionary. CMPEs have immense riches to give humanity both in terms of the guidance they have to offer and in terms of what their existence implies about the nature of reality. In the end, they offer concrete evidence for the existence of a higher plan for human life, and, in my view, even for the existence of a higher Planner (I'll discuss these points in the final chapter).

Interestingly, this paragraph was basically a distillation of "Full Circle" and "Science to Discover God's Plan." So, just as with the previous sign, I was trying to bring the message of "Full Circle" into this book, and writing about my plan to bring it into this current chapter, and here again I had a sign backing that up.

Also, notice how CMPEs were depicted here. The symbol for my book was *The Journey That Never Was*, a book about accessing guidance from the Holy Spirit. So that is how the signs were symbolically portraying themselves here—as guidance from the Holy Spirit.

The Truth of Symbolism

We saw something strikingly similar in "The Truth of Symbolism," from Chapter 6. Whereas "The How-to Component" likened signs to guidance from the Holy Spirit, "The Truth of Symbolism" likened them to Bible stories, stories that carry a message for our lives and that, of course, have traditionally been seen as inspired by God. This was a very minor note in the sign, but set next to the other signs, it stands out.

Nice Day

Finally, there was the last CMPE I had about this book, which was "Nice Day" in Chapter 9. This one didn't say the source of signs was God, but it did liken their source to a car salesman who is so intent on making the sale that he loses no opportunity to push for it. In other words, it characterized CMPEs not as the product of impersonal law, but as the expression of a communicator, one who has an overriding agenda of getting across his big message. (However, please don't mistake me for saying that I am likening God to a car salesman!)

The picture created by all five signs together

So, there have been five CMPEs about this book. Here they are, in the order I have just presented them:

1. Full Circle (Chapter 11)
2. Science to Discover God's Plan (Chapter 11)

3. The How-to Component of this Book (Chapter 1)
4. The Truth of Symbolism (Chapter 6)
5. Nice Day (Chapter 9)

These five signs end up being a remarkably interrelated cluster. They are a classic example of how different signs on the same subject will add up to a single larger picture. Let's look at that picture, by including any theme that occurs in at least two of the signs (leaving out the writing themes we explored in Chapter 7). In the following paragraph, each sentence is built around a theme that shows up in two or more of the five signs:

> I am either working on (2, 3, 4, 5) or writing about (1) this book. Specifically, I am trying to include in it the themes from "Full Circle," and am stating my intention to explore those themes in full in this chapter (2, 3). I then encounter another book (3, 4) or some other material (1, 2, 5) that is so parallel to what I wrote that it makes for a CMPE. This CMPE backs up my idea that signs provide physical evidence for God or for God's plan (1, 2, 3). They are thus a case of the scientific spirit leading to evidence for a religious worldview (1, 2). As such, they have real potential importance for the world (1, 2, 3) and should have a book written about them (1, 2). The symbolism in this sign depicts signs as a case of someone speaking, either God (1), the Holy Spirit (3), or an unidentified speaker (5); someone with a "plan" (1, 2, 3) or "big message" (5). This same symbolism likens signs to something that comes from (or is believed to come from) a divine source: communication from God (1), physical evidence for God's plan (2), guidance from the Holy Spirit (3), or the stories of sacred scripture (4).

As always, the signs maintain a highly consistent stance, which in this case is a stance about themselves. Whatever the actual truth is, *they* clearly think they come from a divine source.

What should we do with this evidence?

I realize that entertaining the idea that CMPEs come from God might be a huge stretch for the critical thinkers among us. Yet as much as this idea may strain credibility, we are still left with a pile of evidence. What are we going to do with it? I sincerely hope there are some who are willing to face and grapple with it *as* evidence. Think about what we have here. We are not talking about private experiences of God. As important as those are, they have been around forever, and while deeply compelling for those who have them, they generally exert little influence on those who don't.

So far as I know, what we have here is something completely new. We have a publicly observable, spontaneously occurring phenomenon, one that could be recorded on camera. It requires no faith assumptions. Rather, it can and should be investigated on its own merits. And though it requires interpretation, instances of it can be interpreted in the same way by different interpreters.

What we then get from this phenomenon is almost beyond belief. We get a concrete, reliable method of identifying what appears to be God's plan for our lives. And we get evidence that something appears to be speaking to us, something that actually seems to be God-like. We get what appears to be physical evidence for God. If we have had a phenomenon like this before, I am not aware of it.

I realize that in the minds of many, such a thing is not even a possibility. We don't even need to look at the evidence, for that would be like taking the time to examine evidence for the tooth fairy. Yet have we so deeply penetrated the secrets of the universe that we *know* that God is impossible, and know this so completely that we can decline to look at possible evidence? That doesn't sound like skepticism to me; that sounds like its own kind of rock-like faith. In an odd sort of role reversal, it sounds suspiciously like the church officials who, as legend has it, refused to look through Galileo's telescope.

If we acknowledge that we haven't gotten to the bottom of the riddle of existence, if we can envision the science and philosophy of ten thousand years from now being profoundly different from that of today, how can we not be open to where further investigation of this phenomenon might lead?

That, I believe, is all we need at this point: to open an investigation. Obviously, one person stepping forward with stories from his life and the lives of people he knows is not enough to establish anything. I have drawn some conclusions in these pages, but as I have said, they assume that my experience over the last thirty years will hold true on a more general level. If my conclusions will ever become broadly credible, it will be because they have been supported by a variety of researchers drawing on the experiences of thousands of people.

This phenomenon is eminently open to investigation. If my experience is anything to go by, then CMPEs are occurring in ordinary lives all over. We can't make them happen on demand, but we could set up procedures to accurately record them. This could even include catching them on film. True, the fact that each CMPE needs interpretation could lead to the chaos of endless conflicting interpretations. Yet, as I mentioned above, my experience is that different researchers can independently arrive at the same interpretations of particular signs. Just as we can agree on what "Call me tomorrow at 9 a.m." means, so we can agree on what a particular CMPE means.

These researchers, like any researchers, would have to be gifted and well-trained. This is a phenomenon that is open to tremendous misunderstanding and misuse. Every step along the way is fraught with potential error, from spotting a possible CMPE, to accurately recording it, to verifying that it is a CMPE, to identifying the parallels and the subject situation, and finally to interpreting its message. A good researcher would need to be intelligent, experienced, and above all, have an honest mind. In the hands of those lacking these qualities, research into this phenomenon would be a disaster. But then, that is no different from any phenomenon. We're not going to ask the janitor to run the particle accelerator, not because he is less of a human being, but simply because this is not where his training and expertise lie.

In the hands of those possessing the qualities I outlined, however, the possibilities are enormous. I don't know if the picture I am about to sketch will happen; I can only share my dream. My dream is that over time, a network of sober, level-headed researchers of this phenomenon arises. These researchers have the exciting task of forging a new discipline, a strange blend of science, social science, and hermeneutics. Their efforts confirm that the phenomenon I have described does indeed happen to individuals all over the world. They confirm that these occurrences do appear to target situations in our lives and do appear to offer perspectives on them. They confirm, therefore, that something—some mind, some force—is weaving the ordinary events of our lives together in ways that "say" something meaningful. They confirm that something appears to be speaking to us.

These researchers look into dozens of fascinating issues. They investigate whether CMPEs happen to certain people more than others, and if so, try to discover why. They use their databases to address the question of whether CMPEs really do convey consistent overall messages. They test to what degree trained interpreters are able to interpret the same CMPEs in roughly the same way. They record predictions made by signs and, once the timetables of those predictions run out, assess how accurate the predictions were. They gather predictions made by CMPEs about collective events, and publish composite predictions of those events.

In my dream, this field gains credibility over time. It evolves; it tightens its methods in response to critics. It therefore becomes slowly but increasingly credible to academics. Eventually, it joins other phenomena in exerting pressure on the reigning scientific worldview, the belief that reality consists only of matter and energy. In such a world CMPEs would not happen, and yet in our world, they do. Indeed, the ever-tighter research makes it reasonable to project that literally millions of them are happening each and every day.

Even if many of the field's researchers remain neutral on the God question, the appearance that this phenomenon comes from God makes it—again, in my dream—a natural participant in the conversation about the existence of God. It makes a very interesting partner in that conversation. Here is a phenomenon that has no connection with faith and tradition, but instead relies on publicly observable events that are directly suggestive of God. This, of course, is a problem for the atheists. But it is perhaps an equal problem for religious institutions. If history is any guide, the last thing the church wants is a God who writes new pages of scripture for each person. A God who can say new things, who can potentially take issue with the church, is not a safe God to have around. I can almost hear the cries: "But wait—God is a matter of *faith*."

In my dream, however, there are some theologians who take note. Just as theologians have had to grapple with the horror of Auschwitz and what that implies about God's activity in the world, so some will also recognize the blessing of CMPEs, and what *that* implies.

Whatever the effect of CMPE research on our view of reality and God, signs will always remain an extremely practical tool. And so my dream is that this field also assists people in using this tool in their own lives. The researchers, then, are also teachers, who conduct classes and workshops in how to spot, record, interpret, and use CMPEs in one's own life. Some of them offer their services as skilled interpreters, who are available to write up detailed interpretations of signs brought to them by people on the street. This is an important service, for while the meaning of many signs is perfectly obvious, others require experience and finesse to interpret, and even many of the obvious ones have deeper patterns that only a skilled interpreter can spot. While helping people in these ways, the researchers also help their own research, for it is through this educational/interpretive function that they gather many of the CMPEs in their database.

Gradually, increasing numbers of people turn to CMPEs to receive guidance for their lives. As these numbers continue to grow, this phenomenon slowly works itself into the fabric of the culture. As a result, the databases of the researchers grow larger and larger, allowing them to more fully explore the overall contours of the philosophy expressed by CMPEs. What is the value system the signs espouse? What do they have to say about business and relationships and politics and spirituality? What do they think about current world conditions? Where, according to them, are we ultimately headed, and how do we get there? People want this information, even people who don't believe CMPEs are from God, for by now it is collectively evident that *something* appears to be speaking to us.

Whatever this voice is—God, extraterrestrials, the collective unconscious—how can we not be intrigued? How can we not want to discover its message for us? Thus, as CMPE researchers publish their findings, the signs' viewpoint becomes part of the conversation in our culture, seeping into people's beliefs and values, and inspiring ever greater numbers to work with CMPEs in their own lives. The collective ear becomes slowly but increasingly tuned in this direction.

My dream, in other words, is that one day, in the distant future, we will be able to say that God is speaking, and the world is listening.

Epilogue
God Still Speaks

The previous chapter was always planned to be the conclusion of the book. As it turns out, however, I have one last sign to share. While writing that final chapter, I was fervently hoping for one more CMPE, specifically one that backed up the notion that CMPEs are from God. I thought it would be nice to have a fresh sign about that, as it's been years since one came that stated that as its main point. I have really appreciated the signs that have occurred around my writing of the book. They seemed to me to give you, the reader, a kind of front-row seat for viewing these extraordinary occurrences.

I actually thought that such a sign was fairly likely to happen. But as each writing session passed, no sign came. Finally, I finished the chapter and time was up. No sign. Oh well, I thought, that's how it goes.

Then, about a week later, I ended up spending several hours polishing the chapter, editing it, and incorporating feedback from Nicola. When I finished, I decided to send the chapter to several friends, asking for their feedback. One of these friends was Greg.

Then, thirty-seven minutes later, I received an e-mail from Greg. He was asking for my feedback on the latest installment of his weekly column "Course Meets World." As I read his piece, I saw immediately that here was my sign! His article was so parallel to my chapter, in fact, that I wondered if my chapter, sent a half hour earlier, had influenced it. When I called him, though, he assured me that it hadn't. First, his article had been finished before I sent my chapter out, but he had been unable to send it because of e-mail problems. Second, he had no idea I was even working on that chapter. The last thing he knew was that I had finished Chapter 6, which was months earlier. My chapter, then, had in no way influenced his article.

Here is Greg's article:

God Still Speaks

Source of material commented on:
http://tinyurl.com/2wfwmt

A Course in Miracles tells us that "God's Voice speaks to me all through the day" (W-pI.49.Heading). An essential teaching of the Course is that we should listen to that Voice and let it guide all of our decisions. This guidance needn't take the form of an audible voice: it can come through a thought, an image, a feeling, or myriad other ways. Whatever form it takes, discerning God's Voice clearly on a consistent basis is a skill that won't be learned overnight. Yet the Course promises that, with time and practice, we can hear God's Voice, and that Voice will lead us home.

Hearing God's Voice needn't be anything spectacular. However, sometimes it is spectacular, and I'd like to share a story that sounds pretty spectacular to me. In the evangelical Christian magazine *Christianity Today*, an author who chose to be anonymous (for reasons unclear to me) describes what he calls his "conversation with God."

The story begins with the author meeting 14-year-old twin boys who were the grandsons of an acquaintance. When he first met them, an "inner voice" told him that he would play a significant role in the future of one of the twins, but at the time he dismissed it. Over the next five years, though, he got to know the boys better as they grew into young men, and it turned out that one of them felt a calling to a music ministry. The author, a professor of theology at a Christian university, gave this young man a campus tour, and he immediately felt a pull to attend that university.

There was only one problem: money. His family couldn't afford it, and though he applied for scholarships, he had little success. The author, who is also of modest means, wanted to help him, so one day he prayed: "Oh, God, please use me to make it possible for him to go to this university!" After that, an amazing series of events happened. First, the author got the title for a book in his head. Then he got the outline for it. He started writing rapidly, and in two weeks he had a two-hundred-page manuscript. He sold it to a publisher, who gave him a huge advance, ten times larger than any he had received before. "I felt like I had won the lottery!"

The funny thing was, though, that he had apparently forgotten about his promise to help his young friend. The author needed a new roof; surely the money was for that. God, however, had other plans, and made that clear in the form of an audible voice in the author's head that persisted for several days. The conversation went like this:

God: "It's not your money."
Author: "What do you mean it's not my money?"
God: "It's not your money. It's his."
Author: "Whose?"
God named the young man who wanted to go to the university.
Author: "All of it?"
God: "That and the rest" (any future royalties the book might make).
Author (shaking his fist in the air): "What about my roof?"
God: "I'll take care of your roof, if you'll be obedient."
Author: "If you want to use me to help him go to the university, why not give me everything it will cost? Why this amount that will make a difference but not pay his whole way?"
God: "Others have to be obedient too."

To make a long story short, the author followed God's guidance and everything fell into place. Financial aid began pouring in for the young man from a number of sources—apparently the others who needed to be "obedient" had been—and he was able to attend the university. The author even got his new roof. And when he shared with the young man everything that happened, the young man choked up with tears. He had been wrestling with doubts about his calling, but now he felt that the author's story was a confirmation of his call.

It's difficult to tell with absolute certainty whether guidance comes from God. The author himself says he is usually skeptical about such things, which I think is a good stance to take. But this incident has a number of elements that in my experience seem to be signs of real guidance. The author asked God to help another person. This caused something—the book—to drop into his mind out of the blue. The guidance he received about the money was counter to his own desires and expectations. Throughout the process, you really get the sense that God had a plan in mind and things were arranged. And in the end, the guidance helped everyone involved, including the author himself. He says that even today, reflecting on this event fills him with emotion. For in hearing God's guidance, following it, and giving to his young friend in need, he himself received a precious gift:

> My faith in a living, personal, loving, and providing God has been renewed and deepened. Now I know, more than intellectually, that God still speaks.

This story set alongside my previous chapter is a truly spectacular CMPE. There is an astonishing number of parallels, many of which I am sure you can see yourself. Having surveyed both my chapter and Greg's article, I ended up counting thirty-two parallels! I honestly don't think I've ever had that many before. In that sense, this is—forgive me—an unparalleled sign.

This CMPE is also especially resistant to skeptical criticisms. In terms of the random hypothesis (page 168), it is hard to imagine that two events could just randomly bump into each other and yet share thirty-two parallels, especially of the quality you will see below.

In terms of the unconscious arrangement hypothesis (page 170), it is also hard to see how Greg or I could have unconsciously arranged for these events to come together. All I did was polish my chapter—because I was at that place in my book—and then check my e-mail. All Greg did was write his article—because he had encountered the theologian's recently published story—and then send it off for feedback. He didn't know I was writing this chapter, and I didn't know Greg had encountered this man's story, which I myself had never heard of.

In terms of the inaccurate story-telling hypothesis (page 171), both events were written pieces, which means that memory is not an issue here. Better yet, the events were sent through an Internet Service Provider, which time-stamped them. As a result, both events in their entirety are sitting next to each other in my e-mail program, along with the time and date of their delivery—almost as good as being caught on film. At this point, the only skeptical explanation left that I can see is outright fraud (which would have to include Greg, too, since he will readily verify everything I've said here).

Parallels and interpretation

Now for the parallels. There are so many parallels that I am going to basically talk you through them in groups.

Parallels between my chapter and Greg's article

- Both were pieces written by writers for the Circle of Atonement.
- Each of us was e-mailing our piece to the other asking for feedback.
- Both pieces were about receiving guidance from God.
- Both characterized working with guidance as a skill to be learned over time.[19]
- Both pieces spoke of professional theologians who work with this guidance.[20]

- They both contained a story or stories of guidance from God.

- These stories contained events that were called "incredibly improbable" (my chapter) or "amazing" (Greg's article).

- These stories appeared to be cases of God "speaking."

- Both Greg and I, however, advocated a healthy skepticism toward that idea.[21]

- In the end, however, we both found several reasons to believe the stories may actually be God speaking.[22]

Parallels between myself and the theologian

- Both pieces feature the personal experiences of a particular intellectual—either me (in my chapter) or the theologian (in Greg's article).

- Both the theologian and I teach and write professionally about our religion or spiritual path.

- We both do so at an institution dedicated to it.

- We are both theologians, at least in the broadest sense of the word (I am not a credentialed theologian, but I often write about theological topics).

- Both of us, however, have stepped outside our usual professional activites to write about our personal experience with divine guidance.

- We don't always like what this guidance has to say.[23]

- In the experiences we relate, we are both guided to write a book.

- According to the guidance, the book is intended to help a specific audience.[24]

- With this audience, it has the effect (or is meant to have the effect) of quelling their spiritual doubts.[25]

- We both adopt an unusually skeptical stance for writers on religion and spirituality.

- Yet our stories contain such tangible evidence that we are won over.

- In the end, both of us profess experiential conviction in God speaking.

Parallels between the theologian and Agent Scully (from the "Full Circle" sign)

- Both the theologian and Agent Scully have a highly rational mindset that has historically led them to explain away contemporary events that appear to be miraculous or paranormal.[26]

- Yet in spite of this skepticism, both now personally witness miraculous events that renew their faith.

- This leads them to express, as their concluding line, their belief that "God is speaking" or "God still speaks" in the world today.[27]

- And this concluding line becomes the central as well as the climactic line in both my chapter and Greg's article.[28]

Parallels between God as revealed in my chapter and in Greg's article

- Both pieces call this God "loving."[29]

- Both say this God has "a plan."[30]

- As part of this plan, physical events are "arranged."[31]

- This plan is for our own lives, yet is clearly interwoven with the plan for the lives of others.[32]

- It asks us to reach out toward others with helpfulness, to a degree that often goes against our wishes.[33]

- Yet this ends up being in our best interests, for the sake of our own welfare.[34]

This is an incredible list of parallels. It's not just the number of parallels that leaves me impressed, it's also their quality. First, most of the parallels involve central, rather than peripheral, elements in the two pieces. Second, the parallels as a whole possess a remarkable unity. They repeatedly present us with different permutations of a single image: *a person who is dedicated to rationality and intellectual caution, yet who is faced with and persuaded by tangible evidence that God is speaking.*

We have me as an example of that, in my parallels with both the theologian and Greg. We have Greg as another example. He is cast as an author who advocates caution toward the idea that God is speaking, yet finds several reasons to believe a particular story is an example of just that. We have, of course, the theologian, the key symbol in this sign. And we also have the character of Agent Scully. Between them, these four figures soak up the majority of the parallels.

Thus, the parallels are dominated by four different versions of the exact same pattern. How can that be chance? How can we not see some kind of intelligence operating here?

In light of these parallels, what, then, should the interpretation be? On the most basic level, since the subject situation is clearly the chapter I wrote, the sign is confirming the essential rightness of that chapter. Specifically, it is confirming that CMPEs really do provide physical evidence for a loving God. They provide concrete support for the existence of God's plan, a plan that can impress itself onto the events of our lives, and that weaves each life into the plan for other lives. The objectives of this plan often run counter to our wishes. It often asks us, for instance, to reach out and help more than we think we can. But in the end, the plan is about our welfare. God really is looking out for us.

What especially interests me, however, is the content added by that repeating pattern of four individuals. That pattern says that *because* CMPEs offer physical evidence for God speaking, they can be particularly helpful for people with a rational, scientific bent, people who *need* physical evidence. Perhaps, like the theologian, these people believe in God, but just doubt that God really acts in the world anymore. Perhaps, like Scully, their skeptical mindset has undermined their faith in God altogether. Or perhaps, like Greg and me, they are simply unwilling to believe without solid, material support for their beliefs.

Whatever the case, CMPEs can provide them with the evidence they need. This may happen through them learning about CMPEs, yet there is a special focus here on them having their own personal experience. The theologian, Scully, and I all directly experienced events that looked like God speaking to us. That direct experience is what we found so convincing. So the implication here is that people with that rational, scientific bent will begin experiencing (more accurately, *noticing*) their own CMPEs.

The result is that they may be affected by CMPEs in the same way I have been. Like me, they may become convinced God is actually speaking to them. They may find their faith confirmed. Or they may be affected by CMPEs like the theologian was by his experience of hearing God. Like him, they may come to know, more than intellectually, that God still speaks. They may find their faith renewed. Finally, they may be affected by CMPEs like Scully was by her witnessing of miracles. Like her, after a long journey away from God, they may come full circle. They may find their faith restored.

And that is why this book needs to be written. It showed up in event 1 (my Chapter 11), where I related how the signs guided me to write it. And it showed up symbolically in event 2 (Greg's article), which told of how the theologian was also guided to write a book. If we place these references to the book next to what the rest of the sign says, the implication is that this book is needed as a vehicle to reach people who are like the four individuals in this sign.

Connection with previous signs about this book

Another impressive feature of this CMPE is that it is astonishingly similar to the five earlier signs about this book. It is no exaggeration to say that it is virtually a summary of them. Indeed, if you take my summary of them from the previous chapter, snip out a few details and soften a couple of points (the ones in brackets), the result is a description of *this* CMPE:

> I am...working on...this book. Specifically, I am trying to include in it the themes from "Full Circle," and am...explor[ing] those themes in full in this chapter [Chapter 11]. I then encounter...some other material that is so parallel to what I wrote that it makes for a CMPE. This CMPE backs up my idea that signs provide physical evidence for God or for God's plan. They are thus a case of the [rational, empirical] spirit leading to evidence for a religious worldview. As such, they have real potential importance for [a certain type of person] and should have a book written about them. The symbolism in this sign depicts signs as a case of someone speaking, either God...or...some-

one with a "plan"....This same symbolism likens signs to something that comes from...a divine source: communication from
God, physical evidence for God's plan.

You really have to wonder: How could two events stumble into each other
and just happen to produce a sign that is *this* similar to previous signs on
the same topic? It either stretches the laws of probability to the breaking
point, or it implies some sort of unified mindset running through all six
signs.

Conclusion

It is this remarkable consistency between this final CMPE and the
previous ones about this book that has sparked for me a new perspective on
all of them. In hindsight, I am amazed that I didn't spot it a long time ago.

Let's go back to "Full Circle," the CMPE that started it all and that several
of its successors refer back to. That sign said, in part,

> By employing the same mindset that has brought our Western
> world away from faith in a loving God, the signs have the poten-
> tial to bring people full circle. They really do have potential
> importance for our world. It is therefore a good idea for me to
> write a book about them and try to have it reach a large num-
> ber of people.

Now, in my mind, the import of this CMPE was mostly about me: "You
need to write a book about signs and try to have it reach a lot of people."
This isn't inaccurate, but now I see that it misses the point, because the sign
wasn't really about me, was it? I was just the middleman. The real focus was
the signs talking about *themselves* and the good they can do in the world.
Given that, a more faithful interpretation would surely be the following:
"The signs want to reach people to bring them full circle, and they want to
use you writing about them to do that."

For me, this is a whole new lens through which to see that CMPE, a lens
that seems to fit the subsequent ones as well. For instance, there were those

two signs ("Science to Discover God's Plan" and "The How-to Component of this Book") that confirmed my plan to share in Chapter 11 the message from "Full Circle"—that signs provide physical evidence for God's plan. Viewing these signs through that new lens, I see them as saying, "Yes, it's so important that you include that 'Full Circle' message in that chapter. That's the message we want to get to people."

Then there was "Nice Day" in Chapter 8. This was the one that said, "Yes, [signs] are like that salesman who will use any opportunity he can to get his big message across, even if it doesn't really fit the situation." Here, I did recognize that this CMPE was not just for me. I wrote, "This is a sign that is not so much about my life but about the signs themselves. The signs are telling us how they work." Yet even recognizing this, I didn't connect the dots: "Of course they are telling *us* how they work. That is why they wanted me to write this book in the first place."

Also, when signs happened involving the writing of the book, I thought it was a great stroke of luck, because they gave you, the reader, your own front-row seat for viewing a sign. Now I suspect that this wasn't luck at all. After all, the signs had already said that the book's purpose was to be a vehicle through which they could reach you. Isn't it reasonable to conjecture that those signs were their attempt to do just that? In this vein, it's interesting to note that with every one of those CMPEs, both events were in writing or somehow recorded. This clearly heightened the front-row seat effect, for it enabled you to experience the events directly, through viewing the event material yourself, rather than indirectly through my storytelling.

In other words, I am now seeing several indications that the signs actually have an intention to reach you, the reader. It may seem like a highly questionable move to read intention into happenstance collisions of events. Yet, as we have seen, signs are rife with indicators of intention. In their strongly positive or negative evaluations of situations, they seem to *want* us to go in certain directions. Now I am seeing evidence that they *want* to reach you with news about themselves.

The case for this is greatly strengthened by the final CMPE, "God Still Speaks," for it managed to repeat *all* of the features I just related. First, it virtually duplicated the message of "Full Circle." Second, it confirmed me placing that message in the final chapter (after those two signs had confirmed my earlier plans to do just that). Third, it was another case of the signs using this book to tell us about their nature—in this case, that they come from God. And fourth, it was yet another sign accompanying the writing of this book (with both events in writing, no less), thus affording you, the reader, a front-row seat for watching CMPEs at work. All of this strengthens the impression that the signs really do want to reach you and give you the message that they are physical evidence for God.

Yet this final CMPE did much more than just reinforce the earlier ones. In case you haven't noticed, it basically hijacked the end of the book and made sure it had the last word. I really had little choice in that. Once that sign happened, I *had* to include it. And because it was about the final chapter in its entirety, it had to go *after* that chapter. Thus, once included, this sign *had* to be the last word in the book.

This, of course, only strengthens my sense that I have merely been the middleman through which the signs can reach you. It's as if here at the end of the book they told me to write, as I shared the message they told me to share, they decided that this was the moment they had been waiting for. They moved the middleman to one side and took the stage themselves, grabbing the mike to give you their big message straight from their own mouth.

In the process, they seemed to display actual dramatic flair. They not only arranged to have the last word, but what a last word! This CMPE is a perfect specimen. It is frankly one of the most impressive and amazing CMPEs I have ever had. The other signs I had while writing this book were quite average, but not this one. The signs clearly saved the best wine for last.

I realize this all sounds highly speculative, yet my speculations are actually explicitly confirmed in "God Still Speaks." As I mentioned above, the theologian's book clearly functioned as a symbol for my book. And notice how his book was portrayed. The theologian wanted to treat it like it was *his* book, using it to pay for his new roof. Yet he was basically told that it wasn't his book. In the language of his initial prayer, God merely "used" him to write the book, which was really a vehicle for helping the young man, who as a result had his doubts put to rest. Here, in symbolic form, is what the CMPE is saying about *this* book. It is saying that however much I have considered it my book, it is actually something God guided me to write to reach a certain population (those who need to "come full circle"), so their doubts can be put to rest.

I must confess this is a dramatic change in my picture of CMPEs. Without realizing it, I have seen them as mainly responding to specific situations in my life. Something comes up in my life; the signs comment. It seemed as simple as that. I haven't really thought of them as surveying the world situation, noticing conditions that need healing (e.g., people needing to "come full circle"), and then calling specific individuals to provide that healing. And yet, if they really are from God, how else would they behave?

All of this leads me inexorably to one final thought about this last sign. I have presented its message in this way: that through this book and through personal experience, signs will provide people who have a rational, evidence-based mindset with physical evidence that God still speaks. Yet notice how with everything in that message, the CMPE was not only talking about it, but appeared to be *demonstrating* it. It wasn't just *saying* that signs will use this book to reach people; *it* was a sign apparently using this book to reach people. It wasn't just talking about people having their own personal experience of signs; it was giving people something close to their own personal experience. It wasn't just saying that signs provide physical evidence for God; it was itself a classic example of that evidence.

Therefore, if you are someone who has that evidence-based mindset, someone strung uncomfortably between belief and skepticism, could it be that this sign took the stage in order to reach you? Could it be that it showed up in such a dramatic, climactic way in order to give you the evidence you have been looking for, concrete evidence that it's not all random, that there really is a purpose and a plan? And could it be that as it gave its message, it wasn't just saying that God still speaks, but was itself a demonstration of that? Could it be that before your very eyes, in a scientific age in which such a thing seems impossible, God spoke to you?

Endnotes

1. Barbara Harris (Whitfield) and L. Bascom, *Full Circle: The Near-Death Experience and Beyond* (New York: Pocket, Simon and Schuster, 1990).

2. Barbara Harris Whitfield, *The Natural Soul* (Pittsburgh: SterlingHouse Books, 2009).

3. Robert Perry, *Path of Light: Stepping into Peace with 'A Course in Miracles'* (Sedona, AZ: Circle Publishing, 2004).

4. Helen Philips, "Paranormal Beliefs Linked to Brain Chemistry," *New Scientist*, 27 July 2002.

5. C.G. Jung, *Synchronicity: An Acausal Ordering Principle* (Princeton, NJ: Princeton University Press, 1960), p. 22.

6. Synchronicity, p. 109.

7. Synchronicity, p. 109-110.

8. Synchronicity, p. 23.

9. Craig S. Bell, *Comprehending Coincidence: Synchronicity and Personal Transformation* (West Chester, PA: Chrysalis Books, 2000), p. 54.

10. Ray Grease, *The Waking Dream: Unlocking the Symbolic Language of Our Lives* (Wheaton, IL: Quest Books, 1996), pp. 1-2.

11. Marcus J. Borg, *The Heart of Christianity: Rediscovering a Life of Faith* (San Francisco: HarperSanFrancisco, 2003), p. 49.

12. Heart of Christianity, p. 54.

13. To be fair to Borg, he doesn't see biblical stories as communications from the divine, but rather as a cultural product of a human community.

14. Linda Acredolo, Ph.D, and Susan Goodwyn, Ph.D, *Baby Signs: How to Talk with Your Baby Before Your Baby Can Talk* (Chicago: Contemporary Books, 2002), p. 107.

15. Mark Henderson, *The Times Online*, May 18, 2006 (http://www.timesonline.co.uk/article/0,,3-2185477,00.html).

16. Mark Egan, "Congress is pressed for bailout with dire warnings," Reuters, September 24, 2008 (http://www.reuters.com/article/ousivMolt/idUSTRE48N7RE20080924).

17. Michael T. Burcon in Jack Canfield, et al., *A Cup of Chicken Soup for the Soul: Stories to Open the Heart and Rekindle the Spirit* (Deerfield Beach, FL: Health Communications, Inc., 1996), pp. 130-131.

18. This point is made by Jesus scholar John Dominic Crossan.

19. Event 1: "The researchers…conduct classes and workshops in how to spot, record, interpret, and use signs in one's own life." Event 2: "Discerning God's Voice clearly on a consistent basis is a skill that won't be learned overnight. [It takes] time and practice."

20. Event 1: "There are some theologians who take note. Just as theologians have had to grapple with the horror of Auschwitz and what that implies about God's activity in the world, so some will also recognize the blessing of signs, and what *that* implies." Event 2 is about a theologian who is following dramatic guidance.

21. Greg: "The author himself says he is usually skeptical about such things, which I think is a good stance to take."

22. In event 1, I listed a number of reasons why God appears to be the best explanation. In event 2, Greg said, "But this incident has a number of elements that in my experience seem to be signs of real guidance"—meaning, guidance that really came from the divine.

23. Event 1: "I don't always like what they have to say." In event 2, the man's dislike of giving the money from the book for the young man's college education was a key feature of the story.

24. Event 1: My book was meant to help those needing to "come full circle." Event 2: The theologian's book was meant to help the young man.

25. Event 1: The "Full Circle" sign said the book would bring about a "return to a traditional faith in God speaking." Event 2: "[The young man] had been wrestling with doubts about his calling, but now he felt the author's story was a confirmation of his call."

26. Event 2: In his own article, the theologian stated that he's skeptical about "things supernatural" and doubts "most miracle stories except the ones in the Bible."

27. Scully: "Afraid that God is speaking…but that no one's listening"; theologian: "Now I know, more than intellectually, that God still speaks."

28. Event 1: I repeated several times the line about God speaking but no one listening, making it the basis of my concluding sentence: "My dream, in other words, is that one day, in the distant future, we will be able to say that God is speaking, and the world is listening." Event 2: Greg fashioned his title ("God Still Speaks") out of the theologian's concluding line, which Greg also made his concluding line: "Now I know, more than intellectually, that God still speaks."

29. Event 1: "you obtain evidence of a loving God Who has a plan for the world." Event 2: "My faith in a living, personal, loving, and providing God has been renewed and deepened."

30. Event 1: "a Mind that has a plan for our lives." Event 2: "you really get the sense that God had a plan in mind."

31. Event 1: "a Mind that…arranges events like chess pieces to obtain its objectives." Event 2: "You really get the sense that…things were arranged."

32. Event 1: "Signs seem to come from a mind that has a plan for our lives, a plan that seems to be integrated into its plan for every other life." Event 2: The man's story gave the clear impression there was a plan that was trying to work through him and others, all for the sake of the plan for this young man's music ministry.

33. Event 1: "This…often involves reaching out with helpfulness toward others." Event 2: The guidance received by the theologian was all about helping another person.

34. Event 1: "It seems to have our welfare in mind." Event 2: "And in the end, the guidance helped…the author himself."

About the Author

Robert Perry has taught *A Course in Miracles* (ACIM) since 1986, and in 1993 founded the Circle of Atonement in Sedona, Arizona, which is dedicated to helping establish ACIM as an authentic spiritual tradition.

One of the most respected voices on ACIM, Robert has traveled extensively, speaking throughout the U.S. and internationally. He is the author or co-author of nineteen books and booklets, including the hugely popular *An Introduction to A Course in Miracles*.

Though he has not written about CMPEs prior to this book, he has been working with them and developing his model for them since 1976.

Online Help!

For news and updates on CMPEs, including a free e-newsletter, please visit

www.semeionpress.com.

If you are interested in having a personal sign consultation, please go to

www.semeionpress.com.

Printed in the United States
211204BV00001B/80/P

9 780982 250006